THE KEW GARDENER'S GUIDE TO

GROWING FRUIT

THE KEW GARDENER'S GUIDE TO

GROWING FRUIT

THE ART AND SCIENCE TO GROW YOUR OWN FRUIT

KAY MAGUIRE

FRANCES LINCOLN

Contents

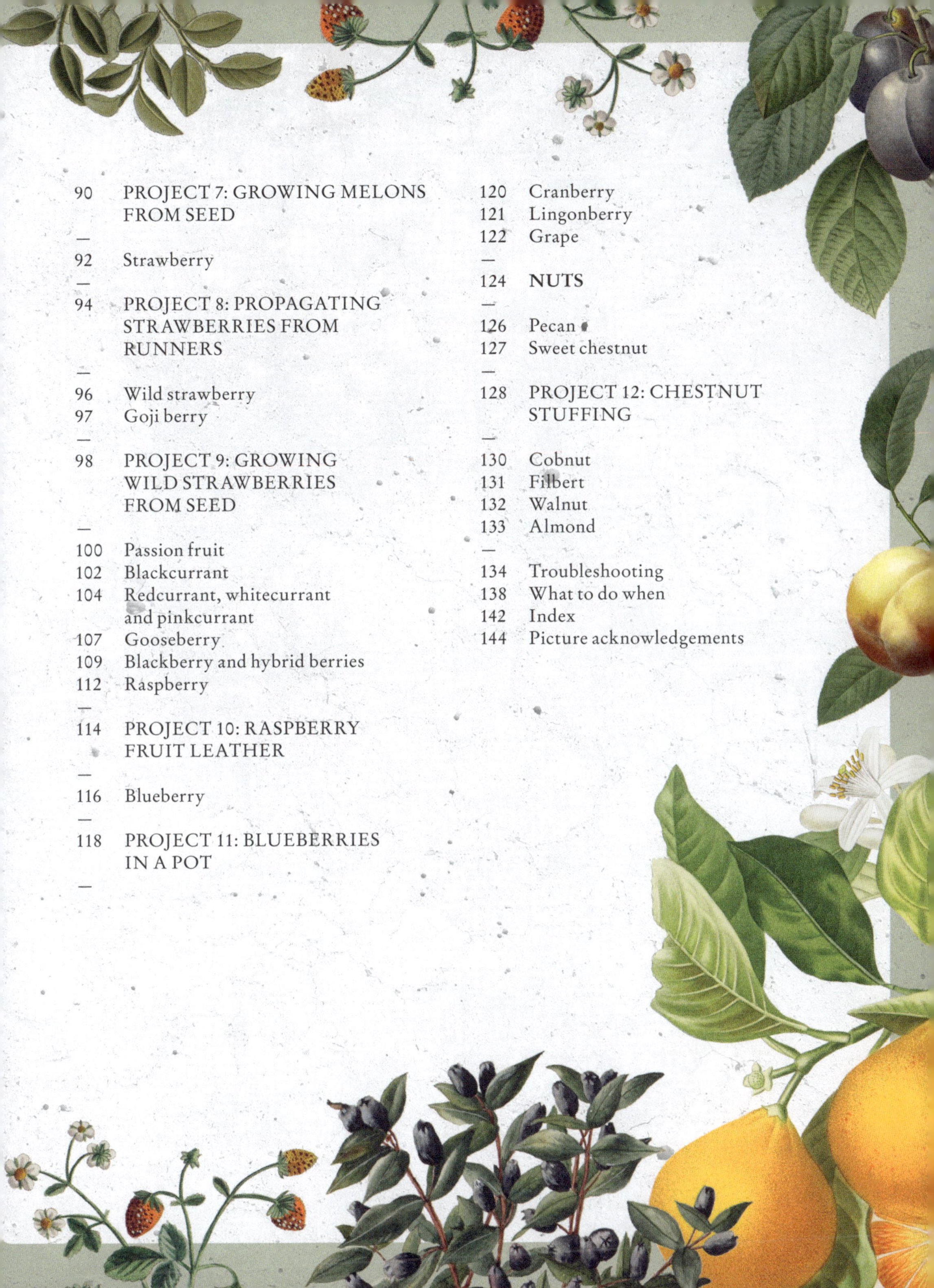

Introduction to growing fruit

—

THE VALUE OF FRUIT

Since the earliest hunter-gatherers first plucked berries from the trees and shrubs around them, humans have adored fruit. Designed by nature to be attractive and delicious so that birds, mammals or insects would eat it and so spread its seed, humans too discovered its sweet, delicious juiciness – and, once tried, it was never forgotten. Fruit is a delight and a treat, and we have been eating and enjoying it for thousands and thousands of years.

It is also incredibly good for us. Fresh fruit is not only bursting with essential vitamins, minerals and antioxidants as well as fibre, but it also tastes completely different when freshly picked and warmed by the sun than it does when bought off a supermarket shelf. Nothing can compare with the fragrant sweetness of a just-plucked strawberry or the tart plumpness of a home-grown cherry. Even the relatively common and humble apple becomes a whole new taste experience when you try your first, delectable harvest.

Fruit is versatile, too, being easily preserved in pickles, chutneys and jams (see Making quince jelly, page 48), dried (see Perfectly preserved dried fruit, page 82), made into fruit leathers (see Raspberry fruit leather, page 114) or bottled into delicious liqueurs (see Making damson gin, page 74). Therefore, even when the harvest is over, you can savour the taste and aroma of summer for months, if not years, to come.

Most fruit plants are perennials. The cost of a tree or a bush is considerably more than a packet of vegetable seed, and it can also take a little while to become productive, so it is worth putting some time and thought into what you wish

OPPOSITE LEFT Fruit is easy to grow and beautiful, blending well with ornamental plants in the garden.
OPPOSITE RIGHT A fruit tree may appear expensive to buy, but it will reward you with produce for many years to come.
LEFT No matter where you live, delicious home-grown strawberries can be grown easily in a hanging basket.

to grow before you start planting (see Before you start, page 18). Fortunately, there is no specialist knowledge or skill required to succeed. After the initial outlay of energy and expense, most fruit will reward you with free harvests for many years to come. Once planted, fruit is easy to look after – there is none of the constant toil and tilling that goes with vegetable growing, and no need to keep sowing every year as you would when growing annual vegetable seed. Shop fruit is also expensive to buy and is very often imported, so you will make savings to your carbon footprint as well as your pocket.

There is a fruit that grows in just about every situation and condition to be found in a garden, so there truly is something for everyone. And if space is limited, dwarfing rootstocks (see Rootstocks, page 14) and compact varieties mean that even the smallest garden or balcony can accommodate a tree or shrub in a pot, and everyone can enjoy a little home-grown fruit at some point in the year. At the other extreme, if you have the space and plan carefully, you can eat your own freshly grown fruit every single month of the year.

Wherever you garden, start by growing the fruit you love to eat – be it a luscious fig or a tart lime – and it is unlikely you will want to stop. Fruit is an integral part of our lives and growing your own is a joy. This book explains the many different types and needs of fruit and helps you to identify those that will grow best in your garden, greenhouse or conservatory. It gives you the inspiration and help you need to get going and to ensure that you continue to keep your fruit happy, healthy and providing delicious harvests year after year.

Tree fruit such as plums are crops that grow naturally as trees and, now, thanks to modern rootstocks and self-fertile varieties, even the smallest space can support at least one.

Soft fruit includes cane fruit and bush fruit such as these redcurrants, as well as strawberries.

THE RANGE OF FRUIT PLANTS

Fruit comes in all plant types, sizes and forms. Unlike vegetable plants, most fruit is perennial – either a woody shrub or tree, climbing vine or herbaceous perennial, which means that it has a longevity you would not find in the vegetable garden. When you buy a fruit plant it is an investment that will reward you, and often future generations, with a bounty of delicious fruit each and every harvest.

Types of fruit

One of the main types of fruit are those that grow on trees. Often referred to as top fruit, these either have a central stone (as with plums, apricots, peaches and cherries) or a core with pips (as with apples, pears and medlars; also known as pome fruit). In a separate category, nuts are trees that produce fruit with a hard, outer shell surrounding an inner, edible kernel; these include almonds, walnuts and cobnuts.

Soft fruit includes all bush fruit (such as currants and gooseberries), cane fruit (such as raspberries and blackberries) and small herbaceous plants (such as strawberries). Finally, there are also vines and fruiting climbing plants (such as kiwi fruit, grapes and melons).

RIGHT ABOVE Apricots are one of a few fruits that need a cool winter to flower and fruit well.
RIGHT BELOW Hailing from the Mediterranean, melons must have a long, hot summer to produce a good crop.

Hardiness

Fruit plants hail from all over the world and are native to a whole host of different countries and climates. It is, therefore, unlikely that everyone can grow every fruit they might wish to. Very few fruit will produce a harvest in all climatic zones and the cold hardiness of fruit crops can vary widely. Some can tolerate a light frost for just a few hours; others such as apples, apricots and strawberries can cope with long periods of freezing and actively need a period of winter chilling, while fruit such as watermelon and citrus depend on a long season of high temperatures to grow, develop and ripen fruit.

For those living in zones 2–7, the first thing to establish is whether the fruit you wish to cultivate is able to grow outside through winter without harm. If not, a greenhouse can help to expand the range of plants you can grow – a heated greeenhouse even more so. Different techniques such as cloching and protecting plants with fleece will also help to increase the types of crops you can grow or to extend their season of harvest.

Hardiness zones

Each fruit entry has a hardiness zone rating, as classified by the Royal Horticultural Society (RHS), which indicates the range of temperatures (from hot to freezing) that each particular plant tolerates. Plants in zones 1–2 require frost-free conditions year-round. Plants that can survive a frost are in zones 3 and above, with higher zone numbers indicating a lower temperature below freezing that the plant will tolerate.

For further details of the individual hardiness ratings see the RHS website (https://www.rhs.org.uk/plants/trials-awards/award-of-garden-merit/rhs-hardiness-rating).

TOP FRUIT

Top fruit, or tree fruit as it is also known, describes the biggest and tallest plants in the fruit garden and those that naturally grow as trees. They include apples, pears, cherries, plums, apricots, nectarines, medlars, quince and mulberries, as well as nuts such as almond, hazel and walnut. As well as their delicious harvest, they can also bring height and structure to the garden, and many have beautiful blossom.

Each tree's individual shape and size depends on the rootstock it is grown on (see Rootstocks, page 14), the cultivar and how it is pruned. Most top fruit can be grown as freestanding trees, such as those in an orchard or as a specimen in a lawn, but they can also be trained into a restricted form such as a cordon, espalier or fan (see Restricted tree forms, page 28). Freestanding trees can be grown as dwarf, semi-dwarf and standard trees. Dwarf trees, with their open-centred shapes on clear stems 60–75cm/24–30in long, are perfect for the small garden. Semi-dwarf trees have a taller, clear trunk of around 1.5m/5ft, while the largest – the standard tree – has a clear trunk that is 2m/7ft long and could reach 7m/23ft in total. Standards are only for large gardens or orchards.

Provided that you choose the right cultivar and rootstock, it is possible to find a tree fruit that will suit any garden, no matter what its size – from the largest orchard to a simple container on a balcony.

Apples are one of the most popular top fruit and can be grown in even a small garden if they are trained with care.

Pollination

If space is limited, it is important to remember that many top fruit should be grown with at least one other tree, to ensure fruiting.

For all trees and plants to fruit productively their flowers need to be pollinated – pollen grains from the male anther in the flower must be transferred to the female stigma, and this needs to be carried out either by pollinating insects, such as honeybees and hoverflies, or by the wind.

Some trees and varieties are self-fertile, which means they can pollinate their own flowers, but most need another tree nearby to cross-pollinate their flowers. Therefore, unless there are trees growing in neighbouring gardens, you need the space to grow two trees. Each tree needs to be of the same type of fruit (for example, an apple) but of a different variety that flowers at the same time. This encourages insects to fly from the flowers of one tree to the flowers of the other, transferring pollen as they go.

To make things easy for growers, fruit trees have been classified into pollinating groups. There are seven groups for apples, four for pears and five groups for plums and cherries. When buying your trees, always check whether they are self-fertile and, if not, that both trees are in the same pollinating group.

You can help to ensure honeybees and other pollinating insects visit your garden by growing plants to attract them. These can be native or more exotic plants, but they must be nectar-rich and have simple, single, open flowers that are easy for insects to access.

ROOTSTOCKS

To make it possible for anyone to grow fruit trees, they are almost always grafted on to different rootstocks. This means that the top of one tree is joined on to the rootstock of another, and it is this rootstock that controls the rate of growth of the tree and, therefore, its size when mature.

In recent years the main research focus has been on breeding dwarfing rootstocks, which result in smaller trees that fruit earlier in life than they would otherwise, making them more productive. The type of rootstock you need depends on the size you want your tree eventually to become and whether you want to train your tree – some rootstocks are more suitable for particular types of training (see Restricted tree forms, page 28).

Unhelpfully, rootstocks have names that do not relate in any way to their size or productivity; instead, they are usually a sign of where they were developed.

Apples

There are more rootstocks for apples than for any other type of fruit trees. The main ones suitable for growing in small gardens are M27, M9 and M26.

BELOW LEFT Almost all tree fruit are grafted, making it possible for you to grow small productive trees.
BELOW RIGHT Different rootstocks affect the size of the mature tree so choose exactly the right size plant for your space.

M27 is a very dwarfing rootstock, with trees reaching around 1.8m/6ft, and is perfect for cordons (see Restricted tree forms, page 28). Although small, M27 trees should not be grown in pots as this puts them under considerable stress. All trees need to be staked permanently.

Trees on the dwarfing rootstock M9 reach 2–3m/7–10ft; they are ideal for containers, cordons, fan training and bush trees. All forms need permanent support.

M26 produces semi-dwarf trees, 3–4m/10–13ft tall, and is good for cordons, espaliers and fan training as well as containers. Trees with this rootstock should need staking for only the first couple of years.

MM106 and MM111 are more vigorous rootstocks, growing to 4–5m/13–16ft, while M25 reaches 5–6m/16–20ft. They are often used for fans, espaliers, half-standards and bush trees in large gardens, paddocks and orchards.

Pears

Quince C and Quince A are the best choice for pears grown in a garden. Quince C is semi-dwarfing, reaching 2.75m/9ft, and is good for cordons,

BELOW LEFT Pears are best grown on quince rootstocks, which are more dwarfing and earlier cropping than pear rootstocks.
BELOW RIGHT Whichever rootstock you choose, your pear will need staking for at least five years.

containers and vigorous varieties. All trees need permanent support.

Quince A is a semi-vigorous rootstock, producing trees around 3.5m/12ft tall; these should need staking in only their first five years. This rootstock is suitable for fans, cordons, espaliers and half-standards.

Cherries
Sweet cherries are vigorous trees and potentially the largest of all the fruit trees grown in gardens. They are best trained as fans if space is an issue. Acid cherries are less vigorous and can be grown as bush trees or fans.

The semi-vigorous Colt rootstock is best for fan training both acid and sweet cherries. Trees reach heights of 4m/13ft and are best for orchards and large gardens. Gisela 5 (G5) is the best semi-dwarfing rootstock for cherries, with plants reaching just 3m/10ft. Unfortunately, only a handful of varieties can be grown on it is including the sweet cherry 'Stella' and the acid cherry 'Morello'. All trees need staking

Plums, gages and damsons
The plum and damson dwarf rootstock VVA1 is perfect for containers and small trees, with plants reaching just 2.5m/8ft. Pixy produces trees 3–4m/10–13ft tall and is good for bush trees, cordons and fans. Trees need staking in their first four years.

St Julien A is the most widely used plum rootstock, and its trees reach heights of 4.5–5m/15–16ft. They can be used for half-standard, bush and fan-trained trees. St Julian A trees produce fruit a year later than those grown on a Pixy rootstock.

Peaches, nectarines and apricots
Both VVA1 and St Julien A rootstocks are widely used for peaches, nectarines and apricots, which are all closely related to plums.

SOFT FRUIT

Soft fruit is the term that encompasses all fruit that are not trees. It includes bush fruit, which comprises compact, shrubby bushes such as gooseberries, blueberries and red-, white- and blackcurrants, as well as cane fruit such as raspberries and blackberries. Bush fruit can be trained into different forms and can develop fruit either on the current season's wood or on the following season's, depending on type. Most cane fruit develops its canes in one year and fruits in the next year at the same time as producing new canes, which will fruit the year after that.

Strawberries are also included in this group. These small, bushy herbaceous plants die back each autumn and reappear again in spring, fruiting later in that season.

Most soft fruit plants are versatile and can be grown in dedicated cages, trained against walls or fences or easily mixed in an ornamental border. Many can be grown in containers – provided that the right variety is chosen – and strawberries thrive in a window box or hanging basket. Almost all soft fruit plants are self-fertile.

Cherries are naturally large trees and one of the earliest fruit trees to ripen in summer.

BEFORE YOU START

Before you decide which fruit you are going to grow, you need to know what your garden or growing space is like. Factors such as its soil, the levels of sun and shade, frost pockets and exposure to the wind all influence the fruit crops you can grow. It is essential to know and understand your garden, to avoid growing trees and plants that will struggle. Therefore, spend some time in your garden getting to know it, noting how the sun moves across the space, the areas of damp or dry soil, where shadows fall and where the frost is last to melt.

Soil

All new plants each need to be given their optimal spot to thrive as fruit crops are predominantly perennial plants, and, therefore, in the ground for many years, it is crucial they are planted in the right spot from the start.

Knowing what type of soil you have means understanding both its texture (whether it is sandy or clay) and its pH (is it acid or alkaline?).

Most fruit crops require fertile, well-aerated soil with a neutral to slightly acidic pH (pH 6–7). You can assess your soil pH with a simple home-testing kit from a garden centre. This will help you establish whether you need to adjust the pH to suit your crop, but there is only so much you can do in that way. If your soil is at either end of the pH extreme for that particular fruit crop, it may be easier to choose something else or grow certain crops such as acid-loving blueberries in ericaceous compost in a pot instead.

Soil drainage is also important and is intrinsically linked to the type of soil you have – and whether it is made up of clay, loam or sandy particles. Clay holds water and nutrients well but can crack in dry weather, while sandy soil is very free-draining, leaching nutrients quickly, but it is earlier to warm up in spring. A loam soil is a mixture of clay, sand and silt and is fertile and easy to work.

Fortunately, all soils – whatever their type – can be improved with the regular addition of organic matter, such as home-made garden compost or well-rotted animal manure, that is dug in or added as a mulch in spring.

Light and warmth

Most fruit plants require at least six hours of sunlight per day. The brightest and warmest spot for your fruit crops is a wall or fence in a warm, sunny position. Here sunlight will help to ripen growth, promote healthy flower buds and produce ripe, luscious fruit full of flavour.

Shelter

Most fruit crops benefit from a sheltered spot well away from high winds, which can damage new growth, flowers and fruit. Such a spot slightly increases the local temperature around your fruit plants, which helps to reduce disease and improves the ripening of new growth and, most importantly, fruit. It is also easier for pollinating insects to reach your plants without having to battle against buffeting winds.

Frost

Frost can be one of the most devastating enemies to the fruit grower, particularly when plants are in blossom, as low

Most fruit crops, even self-fertile varieties, rely on insects to pollinate their flowers, so a sheltered position is essential.

temperatures can kill the flowers and, therefore, your crop.

Fruit have to flower, fruit and ripen all in one year, and many such as plums, pears, peaches and apricots come into flower early in the year. Because an early spring frost can destroy flowers, avoid planting in a frost pocket – areas in the garden where cold air collects, usually at the lowest points such as the bottom of a slope. Instead, position fruit plants on a gentle slope where the frost can flow away. However, always protect particularly vulnerable plants during sub-zero temperatures, by moving them indoors or covering them *in situ* with protective horticultural fleece.

Right plant right place

Once you have assessed your site and know exactly what conditions you have and where, you can work out the plants your garden can grow successfully. The old adage 'right plant, right place' is never truer than when dealing with fruit crops. Matching the crop with your conditions is the only way to ensure a successful and productive harvest, and your growing conditions must dictate the fruit you choose to grow.

Once this is established, the most important factor is then choosing crops you love to eat. Look for your favourite types of fruit and focus on finding varieties that are unusual or impossible to buy in shops.

GARDEN PLANNING

Unless you are lucky enough to have the space for your own dedicated fruit garden or allotment, you will probably have to integrate your fruit crops with your other ornamental and edible plants. Fortunately, many fruit trees and bushes are very attractive in flower: some have gorgeous autumn leaf colour, and it is hard to beat a bush or tree festooned in ripe fruit.

If space is limited, most fruit crops can be grown on dwarfing rootstocks (see Rootstocks, page 14), in containers (see Growing fruit in containers, page 33), or be trained against a wall or garden fence or as a cordon or stepover (see Restricted tree forms, page 28). Family trees, which have two or three different cultivars grafted on the same tree, are also a good option (see Family apple trees, page 62).

Container versus bare-root plants

There are a couple of more options when choosing fruit for the garden, because both trees and bush fruit are sold as containerized or bare-root plants. Containerized plants are available, and can be planted, year-round, while bare-root plants are available only during the dormant season, which is between mid-autumn and early spring.

Bare-root plants will have been lifted from the ground prior to sale and then wrapped in cloth with no soil around their roots. They are much cheaper than containerized plants and there is a wider choice of varieties available.

Container-grown and containerized plants are not the same. Container-grown plants are just that – they have been grown in the pots you buy them in. Containerized plants, however, have been lifted from the ground before sale and then planted in a pot with soil around their roots. Bush fruit are often sold this way in garden centres in autumn, as bundles of plants plunged into pots. They are usually the cheaper of the two container options but are available only during the dormant season.

If you have the space, a dedicated fruit cage will protect your crops from scavenging birds and squirrels.

Shopping

Specialist fruit nurseries run by knowledgeable enthusiasts are the best option when buying fruit trees and plants and will always have the widest choice of varieties and types of fruit. However, unless they are local, you will have to buy online, which means you cannot see the plants yourself. As with other online sources, therefore, you have to rely on trusting the seller, so always choose a reputable company. Traditional garden centres and local nurseries often offer a limited range year-round. Bare-root mail-order fruit plants are available only through the dormant season, while mail-order container plants can be bought year-round.

Always buy plants in the very best condition with lush, healthy foliage, avoiding those with yellow or wilting leaves. Turn a containerized plant out of its pot if possible to check for a healthy root system that is not root-bound. Also avoid plants that are not yet established in their pots, where soil falls away from the root ball. Unpack and check bare-root plants as soon you get them home, and heel them into a bare patch of ground if they cannot be planted straight away.

Check the age of fruit trees, and choose one- or two-year-old trees for most forms or else opt for a three-year-old, ready-trained plant to give you a head start. Feathered maidens, which each have a main stem with side branches, are the best option for growing into bushes, spindles, pyramids and cordons (see Restricted tree forms, page 28). Check the rootstock, too, before buying your tree to make sure you have the correct one for the size of tree you wish to grow (see Rootstocks, page 14).

EQUIPMENT

There is a daunting amount of kit for sale in nurseries and plant centres that is deemed 'necessary' to grow fruit crops. What you actually require depends on what you grow, because top fruit trees need different tools to an annual crop such as melons, for example. Generally, you should invest in just a few key tools to get started.

Whatever you buy, do not scrimp on quality – the cheaper the tool the less time it will last. Instead, check out flea markets and second-hand fairs for good-quality 'vintage' used tools.

The essentials

- Garden fork and spade – for digging holes and cultivating soil.
- Hand tools (trowel and fork) – for planting strawberries and young annuals, and also for weeding.
- A hosepipe – with a spray nozzle for watering.
- Secateurs – for pruning and training.

Useful extras

- Plant supports (canes, stakes, trellis, wires and vine eyes) – for supporting and training fans and espaliers and climbing vines such as grapes and kiwi fruit.
- Garden twine – for tying plants to their supports
- Horticultural fleece or mesh netting – for protecting plants against the cold and pests and diseases.
- Small soft paintbrush – for pollinating plants grown under cover, in windy areas or that flower very early in the season.
- Watering can – with a fine rose for watering young and small plants.
- Fertilizer – most fruit plants need a regular feed using diluted liquid fertilizer or slow-release granules.
- Organic matter (such as home-made garden compost or well-rotted animal manure) – for mulching around the bases of plants to suppress weeds, aid moisture retention in the soil and slowly release nutrients.

OPPOSITE ABOVE LEFT Always ensure that plants are in the very best of health before you buy.
OPPOSITE ABOVE RIGHT A specialist nursery, such as a citrus one, can provide invaluable plant advice.
OPPOSITE BELOW LEFT Although not essential, a small paintbrush is helpful to ensure the pollination of plants in tricky or hard-to-reach spots.
OPPOSITE BELOW RIGHT Secateurs and a pruning saw are important pieces of kit, essential for pruning and training all types of fruit.

PLANTING

The new, young fruit trees and plants that you bring into your garden are vulnerable to a change in growing conditions, and it is essential that you give them the very best start in their new lives. This can be done by providing them with the soil conditions and positions they love. They will then reward you with fruit for years to come.

Containerized plants can be planted year-round but need plenty of extra watering if planted in summer. However, the ideal time to plant is autumn, when the soil is moist and still warm from summer, and plants have plenty of time to get settled before winter cold sets in.

Bare-root plants can be planted at any time during the dormant season, provided the soil is not frozen. Always plant them straight after you get them home; if this is not possible, heel bare-root plants into a bare patch of soil until their permanent site is ready. If the ground is too frozen even for temporary planting, unwrap bare-root plants and water them well once a week until you can plant them in the ground.

Preparing the soil before planting

Clear the site of all weeds, including their roots, as well as large stones, then dig the soil over. If the soil is sandy, poor or very compacted, add a generous layer of organic matter, such as garden compost or well-rotted animal manure, and mix this in, turning it through the soil with a garden fork. Firm down the prepared soil by shuffling over the area with your heels, then rake it level and smooth. Only now it is ready for planting.

Planting fruit trees and soft fruit in the ground

Soak bare-root plants and the root ball of a containerized plant in water for thirty minutes; allow to drain. Dig a planting hole that is the same depth as the root ball and at least three times its width so that the roots have plenty of room to spread. Remove any pot, tease out the roots and place the plant in the hole, making sure the soil-line mark on the stem of bare-root plants or the top of the compost on container plants is level with the soil surface. A stick placed across the hole will help you to get the depth right. Backfill around the roots with soil, firming as you go. Water the plant well.

There is no need to add fertilizer when planting fruit trees and soft fruit. Feeding can actually impede establishment by giving roots less incentive to grow out into the soil looking for nutrients.

Staking

All fruit trees planted in open ground need support to help them stay upright and able to carry their heavy crop of fruit. Therefore, just after planting, insert a short, round stake that reaches just below the crown of the tree – you want to secure only the roots against the wind, not stop the whole tree from moving. Position the stake on the side of the prevailing wind so that the tree sways

OPPOSITE ABOVE LEFT Soak the root ball of a new plant for thirty minutes, before planting.
OPPOSITE ABOVE RIGHT Dig a hole the same depth as the root ball of your plant, and three times the width.
OPPOSITE BELOW Stake a tree just after planting, using a short, angled stake that will secure the roots but still allow the main stem to flex in the wind.

A mulching mat or layer of black plastic will help stop strawberry plants from drying out too quickly.

away from the stake, then knock two-thirds of it into the soil. Secure it to the tree loosely with a padded tie, to prevent the tree from rubbing against the stake.

Mulching

After planting, mulch around the bases of trees and plants, using plenty of well-rotted manure. This helps to keep down weeds and holds moisture in the soil; also, as it breaks down, it slowly releases nutrients. Just keep the mulch away from tree trunks to prevent them from rotting.

Strawberries

Strawberries can be grown just about anywhere. They are very happy in the ground but their compact trailing habit makes them ideal for baskets, pots and growing bags, where they can be easily kept weed-free and away from slugs.

Soak runners in water for a few minutes before planting. If strawberry plants cannot be planted straight away, heel them into an empty bed or keep them in the refrigerator for a few days; just ensure the roots are moist.

Make a small pocket in the soil with a hand trowel. Then plant each runner so that its roots can spread out, and the crown is at soil level. If planted too deep, plants can rot; if too high, they will dry out and die. Firm in and water plants well.

Strawberries are shallow rooting and can dry out quickly, but they also hate waterlogged soil, so water little and often.

GROWING FRUIT IN A RESTRICTED FORM

Fruit can be trained to grow in a range of ways: into a specific shape or in a particular direction, often to save space, to make picking easier or to create an attractive garden feature, as well as to improve productivity. Fruit trees such as apples and pears are the most versatile and easiest plants to train and can be grown in many forms, while all stone fruits and figs can be trained as fans against walls and fences. Some soft fruit such as gooseberries and currants can also be pruned and trained as fans against sunny walls or over arches and trellis.

Fruit trees can be grown in an unrestricted form as a freestanding tree or be trained into a restricted form. When combined with the appropriate rootstock (see Rootstocks, page 14), they can be trained to grow in a container, the tiniest garden or the largest orchard.

Pruning and training often goes hand in hand and the different types of trees grown have individual pruning needs. Unrestricted bushes and trees need very little pruning, spindles require more, and restricted forms such as cordon, fan and espalier need intricate pruning and training.

Freestanding trees

These are the most common form of tree (see Top fruit, page 13), and both tip- and spur-bearing trees can be grown

Training fruit trees such as apricots against a wall makes them easier to protect from early spring frosts.

in this way (see Fruit trees, pages 30–31). Freestanding trees are each pruned in winter (or spring for stone fruits) into a goblet shape with a ring of branches around an open centre.

Restricted tree forms

Restricted-growth trees can take up very little space and are often earlier to fruit and more productive than unrestricted ones. Only spur-bearing varieties can be used to train trees in this way. Once trained, the trees are pruned in late summer, when growth is slowing towards winter and also sunlight can reach into the tree to ripen the wood and promote fruiting buds for the following year.

Cordons are ideal for very small spaces. They are trees planted at an oblique angle of around 45 degrees and produce fruiting spurs along the trunk.

Stepover trees are an attractive way to edge borders and paths and are very low-growing, horizontal cordons on a short stem.

Espalier trees are grown flat against a wall or wire framework and have opposite horizontal branches growing either side of a vertical trunk. They are one of the most elaborate ways to train a fruit tree and, although buying one already trained is expensive, it does save the initial time and effort involved in getting the tree to its initial shape.

A fan-trained tree has branches arranged in a fan shape that radiate roughly from the centre and are tied to wires on a warm wall or fence. Its shape is often used for stone fruit such as cherries, peaches, apricots and plums, as well as for figs.

Spindles and pyramids are both small, freestanding trees that have been pruned and trained into a tapering or cone shape.

Soft fruit

Training helps to maintain the shape of many soft-fruit plants. It also provides support to prevent stems from breaking and snapping under the weight of their fruit and to keep the fruit clean and off the ground.

Cane fruit such as raspberries and blackberries are traditionally trained on wires attached to walls, fences or freestanding posts, but they also look lovely when scrambling over arches, pergolas or trellis, as do kiwi-fruit vines. Bush fruit such as blueberries and blackcurrants do not need training, while gooseberries and red- and whitecurrants are either trained as bushes or else into fans and cordons on wires or against a wall. Grapes are trained along wires and grown as one or more permanent stems with fruiting side shoots growing every year.

OPPOSITE ABOVE An orchard of angled or oblique cordons allows you to cram several fruit varieties into a very small space.
OPPOSITE BELOW LEFT Freestanding trees are one of the easiest ways to grow fruit, requiring less pruning and training than other forms.
OPPOSITE BELOW RIGHT Stepover fruit trees make a beautiful and productive boundary to a border or fruit garden.

PRUNING

Most fruit would survive reasonably well and still produce a crop, if somewhat limited, without being pruned, but for healthy, vigorous, attractive and, most importantly, productive fruit crops pruning is essential. Regular pruning not only removes dead, dying and diseased wood but also lets light and air into the plant. This helps fruit to grow and ripen well and prevents the spread of fungal diseases, which are common when branches are crowded and overgrown. Taking out branches that are crossing and rubbing against others also prevents disease by reducing the chances of wounds developing and infection setting in.

Fruit trees

When a fruit tree is young, it needs formative pruning to guide it into a healthy framework that will produce and carry fruit in the future. Once a tree has matured, it needs regular pruning in winter or summer, depending on its form. Pruning in winter, when the leaves have fallen, allows you to get a clear sense of the shape of a tree but it does promote vigorous trees to put on more active growth than they would if pruned in summer, when pruning restricts growth.

BELOW LEFT Regularly removing some of the older branches allows air and sunlight into a plant.
BELOW RIGHT Prune the new growth of spur-bearing fruit to a couple of buds to form stumpy shoots.

Stone fruit trees such as cherries, plums, peaches and apricots must always be pruned in spring or summer, when they are in active growth, in order to avoid diseases that would enter pruning cuts made in the dormant season.

Most fruit trees develop fruit on spurs or tips, and it is essential to know which your tree does before you prune it. Spur bearers are the most common trees and they bear their fruit on short, stumpy shoots, or spurs, that are usually more than two years old. They require pruning back to these short stumps every year.

Taking out crossing and congested growth opens up the centre of a plant and helps fruit to develop and ripen healthily.

Tip bearers produce fruit on shoots that were produced the year before. They are usually vigorous trees and are unsuitable for training into restricted forms (see page 28) because removing all the fruiting tips cuts out the fruiting wood and so no fruit will be produced. Instead of tipping back, tie in plenty of new shoots for next year's crop.

Soft fruit

Individual soft-fruit plants have their own pruning needs, depending on whether they fruit on the current or previous season's growth. However, all need regular care and the removal of crowded and crossing wood, to create an open, balanced plant.

Cane fruit (except autumn-fruiting raspberries) develop fruit on wood produced in the previous year and, therefore, need pruning every year at the end of summer. All fruited wood is removed down to the ground, and the new wood tied in ready for the next year. Autumn-fruiting raspberries, however, are pruned in very late winter, when all canes are cut down to the ground.

Bush fruit such as red- and whitecurrants and gooseberries should be pruned in early spring, while blackcurrants are pruned every winter.

Grapes are also pruned during early winter.

General pruning tips
Although every plant should be treated individually, the following tips are helpful no matter what you are pruning.

- Always make sure your pruning tools are sharp so that you make clean, smooth cuts. Use the right tool for the job. Forcing the wrong tool to make a cut can irrevocably damage a stem or branch.
- Secateurs are the perfect tool for all stems and branches no thicker than finger width and for nipping out suckers or thinning fruiting spurs. Bypass blades make a cleaner cut than anvil types, which tend to crush rather than cut the wood.
- Use long-handled pruners for branches that are thicker than a finger width.
- A pruning saw is for use on all other branches, stems and trunks that are too thick for secateurs or long-handled pruners.
- A ladder may be needed to reach branches high up in the tree.
- Make all cuts at an angle just above a bud, slanting the cut downwards. If you leave too long a stub it can cause the branch to die back and thus increases the chance of disease.
- Take out all dead, dying and diseased wood first, followed by any branches that are crossing or rubbing against others.
- When removing branches back to the trunk, always leave a small collar to help the tree callus over the wound.
- Remove large or long, heavy branches in stages, to prevent tearing the bark of the trunk.

Keep tools very clean
Stone fruits such as peaches, plums, nectarines and apricots are all prone to silver leaf, while apples and pears are vulnerable to bacterial canker, so make sure all cutting tools are kept thoroughly clean to prevent infection. If you are pruning more than one tree at a time, wipe and clean tools between each tree, to avoid carrying disease from one to another.

By growing tender plants such as citrus in pots, it is easier to move them inside when the temperature drops.

TOP Strawberries are an ideal crop for containers of any kind as they are small and easy to grow.
ABOVE Growbags are ideal for annual crops such as melons. Plant two melons per bag.

GROWING FRUIT IN CONTAINERS

People often think that they require vast amounts of space to grow fruit, picturing endless rows of apples, pears and plums in orchards abuzz with bees or imagining large, walk-in fruit cages full of bushes dripping with berries. However, for many of us the only option is frequently to grow fruit in containers.

Fortunately, almost all fruit trees and soft fruit can be grown in pots, which can be placed on a balcony. In fact, container growing has many advantages and is often a good choice for all of us, not just for those with limited space.

Growing in pots allows you to tailor the soil for plants with specialized needs, such as blueberries which require acidic soil, and to provide better soil if your garden soil is poor. Pot-grown fruit can also be moved relatively simply: into the warmth and sun in spring and summer and out of a frost-prone spot in winter; and it can be more easily protected from pests and diseases. Small trees and bushes can be draped in mesh netting or fleece to protect crops from birds or against the cold, while plants that are small enough, such as strawberries, can be moved indoors to extend cropping at both ends of the season.

Choosing the right container rootstocks
Look for suitable compact cultivars and the right dwarfing rootstocks when choosing a tree. The rootstock helps to control a fruit tree's vigour, and many have been developed specifically for container growing. (See also Rootstocks, page 14.) Look for the following rootstock details on the label when buying your tree:

- Apples – M9, M26
- Pears – Quince C
- Cherries – Gisela 5
- Plums, gages and damsons – Pixy, St Julien A
- Peaches, nectarines and apricots – Pixy, St Julien A

Planting trees in containers
Your fruit tree will be in its pot for a long time so make sure the container you choose is big enough. Look for one that is a couple of sizes larger than the one the tree came in – 40cm/16in in diameter is a good first size. Always put the container in position before you start planting as it will be very heavy to move once planted up.

Use a good-quality, soil-based potting compost, which is heavier and more stable than soilless multipurpose ones; it also holds on to water and nutrients better.

Fill the pot a third full with compost and then set the tree in the pot, making sure it is at the right level – with the soil-line mark on the stem of bare-root plants or the top of the compost on container plants about 3cm/1¼in below the top of the pot. Fill in around the roots with soil, firming it down well until the plant is stable and there is just a small gap between the soil surface and the rim of the container. This will make watering easier. Water the plant in well.

Caring for fruit in containers
Fruit grown in containers will always need more care and attention than fruit grown in the ground. Plants in containers are living off a limited supply of water and nutrients and are dependent on us to ensure these supplies are kept topped up.

Keep an eye on your fruit plants throughout the year. They need watering every day during dry summers and once they start to flower they require feeding with a high-potash fertilizer once a week until the fruit is ripe.

Every two or three years, container-grown trees and perennial plants will need transferring into larger pots filled with fresh compost. Pot them on into the next size up until they reach a pot of 50–60cm/20–24in in diameter. Thereafter, simply give their roots a prune before replanting them back into fresh compost in the same pot. In the years between potting on, give plants a boost by scraping away the top 5cm/2in of compost and replacing it with fresh compost every spring.

OPPOSITE ABOVE LEFT Every two or three years, transfer container-grown perennial crops into a larger pot and fresh potting compost.
OPPOSITE ABOVE RIGHT Check plants grown in pots regularly in summer, watering them every day if necessary.
OPPOSITE BELOW Give container-grown plants the best-quality potting compost; never recycle soil from the garden as it may harbour pests and disease.

Top fruit

Lime

Citrus × aurantiifolia

Family Rutaceae

Height and spread 1–1.5 x 1–1.5m/3–5 x 3–5ft (in a pot)

Hardiness Zone 2

Position Warm, sunny, sheltered and humid

Harvest Winter

There are two main types of lime: acid and sweet. All are pretty, compact, self-fertile plants that grow well in pots and have fragrant blossom. Flowers, small, swelling fruit and ripe fruit often appear on the tree at the same time.

—

WHERE TO GROW

A sunny spot helps to ripen the fruit. In cool-temperate climates, bring pot-grown plants into a greenhouse or sunroom for winter (see also Growing citrus in a pot, page 42). Lime trees prefer fertile, well-drained soil.

HOW TO GROW

Buy grafted plants that are three or more years old. Water plants well, as fruit can drop if it is too dry. Feed year-round with a specialized citrus fertilizer. In cool-temperate areas, keep plants almost dry in winter, and resume regular watering once temperatures rise in spring. Thin out fruit. Re-shape lime trees in winter, to create balanced plants. Pinch out the tips of vigorous growth in summer, and remove any shoots growing below the graft union.

GROWING TIP

Increase humidity around plants by misting with water or by standing plants in pots on trays of moist gravel. Grouping plants together will also help.

DOUBLE ATTRACTION

Limes have a higher content of both sugar and acid than lemons and a distinctive, flowery aroma to their zest.

NOTABLE CULTIVARS

- 'Tahiti', aka 'Persian', has seedless, very tasty, small fruit; plants are very productive.
- 'West Indian', aka 'Mexican', is an acid type with small, rounded fruit and few seeds.

Grapefruit

Citrus × *aurantium* Grapefruit Group aka C. × *paradisi*, pamplemousse, forbidden fruit, pomelo

Believed to be an accidental hybrid between a sweet orange and a pomelo, the grapefruit produces some of the largest fruit in the citrus family, up to 15cm/6in in diameter. Yellow-skinned in colour, its flesh can be white, pink or red and has a taste that ranges from sweet and tart to sour and bitter. Beautiful, self-fertile trees bear glossy evergreen leaves, fragrant blossom and clusters of fruit.

—

Family Rutaceae

Height and spread 5 x 3m/16 x 10ft

Hardiness Zone 1c

Position Warm, sunny and sheltered

Harvest Winter

WHERE TO GROW

Grapefruit needs a frost-free growing spot – above 15°C/59°F – and a long period of warmth and sun for the fruit to ripen. It grows best in a fertile, well-drained spot. In cool-temperate climates, grow in pots indoors (see also Growing citrus in a pot, page 42) and move outside for summer.

CLIMATIC VARIATION

The pink and red pigmentation in the flesh of some varieties occurs when they are exposed to prolonged high temperatures. It should not affect flavour.

HOW TO GROW

Water plants well in summer, ideally with rainwater. In winter keep plants drier, allowing the surface of the soil to dry out before watering again well. Feed plants every week with a specialized citrus fertilizer, year-round. If growing plants indoors, keep the atmosphere humid. Remove the tips of vigorous shoots in summer, and in late winter thin out overcrowded branches and cut back leggy branches by a third.

GROWING TIP

Repot container-grown plants every spring or topdress by replacing the top 5cm/2in of potting compost.

NOTABLE CULTIVARS

- 'Golden Special' (New Zealand grapefruit) bears golden orange fruit.
- 'Marsh' is a free-flowering variety, with seedless, white-fleshed fruit.
- 'Ruby Red' is a large, vigorous tree that produces sweet, juicy, red fruit.
- 'Star Ruby' has juicy, thin-skinned fruit with deep red flesh.
- 'Wheeny' is a vigorous plant, producing lots of large, juicy, sweet fruit.

Orange

Citrus × aurantium Sweet Orange Group, aka *C. sinensis*, sweet orange

Fragrant flowers, glossy, evergreen leaves and distinctive, rounded, bright orange fruit are borne on these lovely, self-fertile trees. Under glass or outside in warm conditions of 10°C/50°F or more, they flower and fruit at the same time. Sweet oranges are usually classified into three groups – Valencia, blood and naval – with the most commercial fruit belonging to the Valencia group.

—

Family Rutaceae

Height and spread
6 x 3m/20 x 10ft
(1.5 x 1m/5 x 3ft in a pot)

Hardiness Zone 3

Position Warm, sunny and sheltered

Harvest
Summer–autumn

WHERE TO GROW

Plant in pots, 50cm/20in in diameter (see Growing citrus in a pot, page 42). Oranges need as sunny a spot as possible to ensure their fruit ripens, and frost-free conditions, so grow them inside or bring them indoors for winter. They prefer a fertile, well-drained spot.

HOW TO GROW

Unless grown as a standard, plants need minimal pruning. Reshape in winter and pinch out the tips of vigorous growth in summer; also remove any shoots below the graft line. Pot on in spring. Water plants well in spring and summer; reduce intervals to every few weeks in autumn and winter. Feed year-round with a specialist citrus fertilizer.

GOOD LUCK
Orange blossom is highly fragrant and traditionally associated with good fortune. Its essence is an important ingredient in the perfume industry.

GROWING TIP

Water plants thoroughly in dry weather, particularly when the flowers and fruit are developing. Increase humidity around plants by misting or standing plants on trays of moist gravel.

NOTABLE CULTIVARS

- 'Baia' is vigorous, with sweet, juicy, seedless naval oranges.
- 'Dwarf Campbell' is a dwarf, early-ripening Valencia orange.
- 'Moro' is a blood orange with distinctive, red flesh; its sweet juice has a hint of raspberry.
- 'Trovita' is heavy cropping and good for eating and juicing; the fruit ripens well in cool-temperate areas.

Growing citrus in a pot

Container growing makes it possible for all of us, no matter where we live, to grow tender fruit. For those living in cool-temperate areas, growing tender crops in pots means this can be done indoors permanently, in a conservatory or greenhouse or in a cool spot in the house such as a porch; or else, during summer, they can be put outside on a terrace or patio and moved inside as soon as the temperatures start to drop.

Citrus are beautiful, small trees with glossy, evergreen leaves and fragrant flowers that blossom throughout the year. However, all are frost tender and most, such as lemons, oranges, grapefruits and limes, need consistently warm conditions with a minimum temperature of 10°C/50°C.

Each plant needs a container at least 50cm/20in in diameter. If you plan to move your plant in and out of shelter, choose a light plastic or fibreglass pot rather than a heavy clay one, to make this annual task easier. Specialized citrus compost is available, or you can make your own using a soil-based potting compost mixed with 20 per cent sharp sand to improve drainage.

In summer water plants regularly, allowing them to drain freely, but in winter keep plants on the dry side, letting the compost dry out between waterings. Citrus are hungry plants and need regular feeding. In summer, when plants are producing green, leafy growth give them a high-nitrogen fertilizer, and in winter, when plants are flowering and fruit is ripening, give them a general-purpose feed. Repot plants in spring or refresh the top 5cm/2in of compost with fresh mix.

1 Citrus are extremely slow-growing plants so improve your chances of getting fruit by purchasing a plant that is at least three years old.
2 Citrus can flower year-round, and fruit can take a long time to mature, so it is not unusual to see plants with both flowers and fruit at the same time.
3 Citrus plants prefer a good weekly drench rather than being watered little and often, even if this leaves the plants a little dry in between watering.
4 Hand-mist around citrus plants during and after flowering, to increase humidity. Standing pots on trays of wet gravel will also help.
5 Citrus plants need minimal pruning, particularly dwarf container varieties. Re-shape plants in winter, and nip out the tips of vigorous growth in summer.

Kumquat

Citrus japonica aka *Fortunella japonica*, cumquat, Chinese orange

Less hardy than some other citrus fruit are kumquats, which bear tiny, orange fruit that is eaten whole; the skin is sweet but the flesh quite sour. Plants are bushy, self-fertile and can be very heavy cropping.

—

Family Rutaceae

Height and spread 3 x 2m/10 x 7ft

Hardiness Zone 1c

Position Warm, sunny, sheltered and humid

Harvest Autumn–winter

WHERE TO GROW

Plants need heat to flower and fruit so are best grown indoors under glass in cool-temperate areas. They need moist, well-drained soil and grow happily in pots (see also Growing citrus in a pot, page 42).

HOW TO GROW

Feed regularly with a specialized citrus fertilizer – reduce feeding to once a month in winter. Water plants well in the growing season – sparingly at other times. Keep plants humid by watering the path in the greenhouse or by misting. Re-shape in late winter or spring. Pinch back the tips of new shoots in summer.

GROWING TIP

Repot plants in spring, into fresh, soil-based compost and a container that is the next size up.

BACK AGAIN

Originally classified as *Citrus*, kumquats were then named *Fortunella* after the plant collector Robert Fortune, who introduced them to the West in 1846. However, they have just recently been reclassified as *Citrus*.

NOTABLE CULTIVARS

- 'Meiwa' bears lots of rounded, tangy fruit.
- 'Nagami' has delicate, bright orange, ovoid fruit.

Lemon

Citrus × limon

Small, aromatic, evergreen trees, lemons have fragrant flowers that blossom whenever conditions are warm, so both flowers and fruit often coincide beautifully.

–

Family Rutaceae

Height and spread 6x1.25m/20x4ft (1–1.5x1–1.5m/3–5x3–5ft in a pot)

Hardiness Zone 2

Position Warm, sunny, sheltered and humid

Harvest Winter

WHERE TO GROW

Lemons need a long, warm, humid growing season – at least six months at 20°C/68°F and a frost-free winter. In cool-temperate regions, grow plants in a container, 50cm/20in in diameter; place it in a warm, sunny spot in summer and bring indoors for winter (see also Growing citrus in a pot, page 42). Lemons prefer a fertile, well-drained spot.

HOW TO GROW

Plants are slow-growing so buy ones that are at least three years old. Water plants well, and feed year-round with a specialized citrus fertilizer. Increase humidity by misting or standing plants on trays of moist gravel. Thin out fruit so that the remaining crop can swell and ripen well. Reshape trees in winter, if required. Pinch out the tips of vigorous growth in summer and remove any shoots below the graft union.

GROWING TIP

In cool-temperate areas, keep plants almost dry in winter; resume regular watering only once temperatures rise in spring.

MEDICINAL WONDER

In 1747 the Scottish physician James Lind, who was a pioneer of naval hygiene, conducted possibly the first clinical trial and subsequently developed the theory that citrus fruit cured scurvy.

NOTABLE CULTIVARS

- 'Garey's Eureka' is hardy to 1°C/34°F, with bright golden, well-flavoured fruit.
- 'Lisbon' is a classic heirloom variety, with medium-sized, tangy fruit with a low seed count and a smooth skin.
- 'Meyer' is smaller and rounder than regular lemons; the fruit is sweet and a deep golden orange; it survives at 5°C/41°F.
- 'Monachello' has rough-skinned, low-acidity fruit with few seeds.

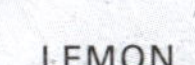

Calamondin

Citrus × microcarpa aka calamondin orange, Panama orange, Philippine lime, calamansi

A cross between a kumquat and a mandarin, calamondins are highly ornamental, beautiful, little trees with glossy leaves, sweetly fragrant, star-shaped flowers and small, rounded, tangerine-coloured fruit. They are also self-fertile, easy to grow and perfect for the first-time citrus grower.

–

Family Rutaceae

Height and spread 2 x 1m/7 x 3ft

Hardiness Zone 3

Position Warm, sun or semi-shade, and sheltered

Harvest Summer–autumn

WHERE TO GROW

Calamondins prefer fertile, well-drained soil. Grow in a container (see Growing citrus in a pot, page 42) in a warm, sunny, sheltered spot and move indoors for winter, or grow them in a conservatory.

HOW TO GROW

Water plants well in the growing season, keeping the soil slightly moist; then reduce in autumn and winter so that the soil dries out between waterings. Keep plants humid: mist them or grow on damp pebbles. Topdress plants in spring. Feed regularly with citrus fertilizer from spring to autumn; feed once a month in winter. Re-shape plants in late winter or early spring. For bushy plants, pinch back the tips of new shoots in summer. Repot plants in spring, into fresh, soil-based compost and a new container that is the next size up.

GROWING TIP

Harvest the fruit as soon as it is ripe. The small, seedy fruit can be bitter when eaten fresh from the tree but is delicious in marmalade or pickled in brandy.

BAD ENVIRONMENT

Despite their ornamental appeal, do not be tempted to grow calamondins in a centrally heated room, because the air would be too dry for them and so desiccate plants.

NOTABLE CULTIVAR

- 'Tiger' has variegated, striped leaves and masses of bright orange fruit on vigorous trees; nip out shoot tips to keep plants in shape.

Quince

Cydonia oblonga

Because it is rarely found in shops, this delectable fruit is worth growing, although it requires patience. Fruits quickly follow lovely pink flowers but need the entire summer until they are ready to pick, still hard and unripe. They then require time to soften and sweeten, releasing their heady fragrance. They are delicious baked, added to apple pies or made into jelly or jams (see Making quince jelly, page 48).

Family Rosaceae

Height and spread 3–5 x 2–4m/10–16 x 7–13ft

Hardiness Zone 5

Position Warm, sunny and sheltered

Harvest Mid-autumn

WHERE TO GROW

Quince loves rich, deep, moisture-retentive soil. Its early flowers are susceptible to frost damage, so give it a warm, sheltered spot.

ROYAL FRUIT

King Edward I introduced the first quinces to England, planting four in the grounds of the Tower of London in the thirteenth century.

HOW TO GROW

When trained as bush trees or half-standards, quinces are easy to grow. They are self-fertile, but will produce a bigger crop if more than one tree is planted. They can be established on their own roots or on a Quince A or Quince C rootstock. Prune in winter to keep plants in good shape, and feed and mulch in spring. Water plants well in dry spells in spring and summer.

GROWING TIP

Leave the fruit on the tree to help it develop a full flavour; then pick and store for 6–8 weeks. Mellowing sweetens and softens the fruit until it is yellow with a sweet and fruity fragrance.

NOTABLE CULTIVARS

- 'Champion' has early-ripening, heavy crops of big, pear-shaped fruit.
- 'Leskovac' bears apple-shaped, early-ripening fruit.
- 'Meech's Prolific' is vigorous and produces large fruit after just three years.
- 'Rea's Mammoth' has heavy yields of very large fruit.
- 'Vranja' bears large, sweet, fragranced fruit; good for cool-temperate regions.

Making quince jelly

Quinces are an old-fashioned fruit, rarely seen for sale in the shops and unknown by many growers, possibly because they are hardly ever eaten raw, fresh from the tree. Quince flesh is yellow, hard and bitter until cooked, when it is transformed into a fragrant, richly flavoured, pink flesh that perks up chutneys, pies and tarts. Quince also contains a very high level of pectin, which means that it is great when making jellies, jams and preserves such as the Spanish quince paste *membrillo*, which is often served to accompany cheese.

To make a simple quince jelly, chop 2kg/4½lb ripe quince and place in a saucepan. Then add the juice and zest of one lemon and just enough water to cover the chopped quince. Bring the mixture to the boil and simmer for an hour or so, until the quince is soft and tender. Then strain the fruit through a jelly bag or muslin; do not press it through. Hang up the jelly bag and leave it to drip slowly into a bowl for at least four hours or, better still, overnight. Return the juice to the saucepan and for every 100ml/3½fl oz of quince juice add 75g/2½oz of sugar. Bring this to the boil, stirring to dissolve the sugar, until it is set. You can test this by putting a little on a saucer and leaving it for a minute. If the jelly wrinkles when touched it is ready. Store your quince jelly in sterilized jars in a cool, dry cupboard, where it will keep for up to a year.

1. Always use ripe, unblemished fruit. Quinces that have a downy skin are still unripe, so leave them to ripen indoors before using them.
2. Once peeled or cut, quinces start to brown quickly so rub them with lemon juice straight away or drop them in water that has a squeeze of lemon juice added to it.
3. Chop the quince roughly before cooking with the lemon, straining the juice and then adding the sugar.
4. Quince jelly is a well-known companion to cheese; it is also lovely just with toast and butter and goes very well with roast lamb.
5. After making quince jelly, do not waste the pulp in the jelly bag. Use it to make *membrillo* by cooking it into a thick paste: add 75g/2½oz sugar for every 100g/3½oz pulp; then chill the paste to set.

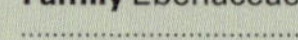

Persimmon

Diospyros kaki aka Chinese date plum, Sharon fruit, kaki

Beautiful, slow-growing, deciduous trees produce shiny, pumpkin-shaped fruit that can be yellow, orange or red. Inside, the smooth, custard-like flesh tastes a little like mango.

–

Family Ebenaceae

Height and spread 12 x 8m/40 x 26ft

Hardiness Zone 4

Position Full sun and sheltered

Harvest Autumn

WHERE TO GROW

Grow in fertile, well-drained soil. Trees need good air circulation: plant freestanding trees away from walls. In cool-temperate regions, grow in a greenhouse or conservatory.

HOW TO GROW

Look for self-fertile varieties and grafted trees for a quick harvest – such trees should fruit within three or four years rather than the more normal seven years. Many other persimmon varieties require a male tree growing nearby before pollination can occur. Persimmon are relatively drought resistant, but need watering in a dry summer. Mulching trees also helps. Do not overfeed plants. In winter, prune young trees to promote a strong framework. Leave the fruit to ripen on the tree, cutting it from the tree with the stalk and calyx still intact. Bring inside to ripen further, to a soft jelly.

SIGN OF THE TIMES

An ancient Chinese tree, the persimmon was chosen by the United Nations to be the tree of peace when it was the sole surviving plant in the nearby country of Japan, after the Nagasaki atomic bomb in 1945.

GROWING TIP

Cold, wet weather rather than low temperatures can kill non-astringent varieties, which demand a dry winter. Astringent varieties are more suitable for cool-temperate, wetter climates.

NOTABLE CULTIVARS

Astringent type

- 'Hachiya' (self-fertile) has acorn-shaped fruit; ripen it fully off before eating.
- 'Tamopan' (self-fertile) bears large, red-orange fruit.

Non-astringent type

- 'Fuyu' (self-fertile) has squat, rounded, sweet fruit that can be eaten before it is fully ripe.
- 'Hana Fuyu' (self-fertile) is a dwarf type, with huge, red-tinged, orange fruit.
- 'Yates' (self-fertile) is a grafted, American variety.

Loquat

Eriobotrya japonica aka Japanese loquat, Japanese plum, nispero, nespolo

Loquats are self-fertile, evergreen trees with shuttlecocks of large, dramatic, corrugated leaves. Scented, cream-coloured flowers in winter are followed by bunches of delicious, pear-shaped fruit – they look a little like an apricot but have a flavour somewhere between a peach and a mango with a hint of citrus.

–

Family Rosaceae

Height and spread 7 x 5m/23 x 16ft

Hardiness Zone 4

Position Sunny and sheltered

Harvest Spring

WHERE TO GROW

Plant in fertile, well-drained soil in a warm, sunny spot. Loquats are best suited to a tropical environment and need a minimum temperature of 15°C/59°F to flower and fruit freely. Therefore, grow under glass in cool-temperate regions.

HOW TO GROW

Water plants regularly in dry periods, and give a high-potash liquid feed every month. Cut back over-vigorous shoot tips in spring and prune out dead, diseased and crossing wood. Harvest when fruits turn a rich, golden yellow and start to soften.

GROWING TIP

White-fleshed fruit varieties such as 'Vista' ripen a little later than other varieties of loquat and are more suitable for cool-temperate or coastal regions.

CONFUSING ORIGINS

Despite its species name of *japonica*, the loquat comes from the cool hill regions of central and southern China. However, it has been grown in Japan for more than 1,000 years.

NOTABLE CULTIVARS

- 'Early Red' bears large, sweet, juicy fruit with white-spotted, orange-red skin.
- 'Kaitaia Gold' is compact, with slightly hairy, yellow fruit that has a good balance between acidity and sweetness.
- 'Mogi' bears firm, golden fruit with a sweet, plum-apricot flavour.
- 'Thames Pride' is a small tree, with abundant, delicious fruit; is less susceptible to caterpillar attack than other varieties.
- 'Vista White' produces pale yellow fruit with pure white flesh.
- 'Wiki Gold' has woolly, white, perfumed flowers and large, golden-yellow fruit.

Fig

Ficus carica aka common fig

Beautifully architectural, self-fertile, small trees or shrubs on which deliciously sweet, distinctive fruit is produced. Figs grow happily outside in cool-temperate climates, provided winter protection is provided and hardy varieties are chosen.

–

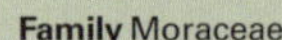

Family Moraceae

Height and spread 3 x 4m/10 x 13ft

Hardiness Zone 4

Position Sunny and sheltered

Harvest Late summer–early autumn

WHERE TO GROW

Figs like good drainage and restricted roots (see Planting a fig, page 54). To ensure ripe fruit in cool-temperate regions, grow in a heated greenhouse or against a warm, sunny, sheltered wall; cover with fleece in winter or move container-grown plants indoors.

HOW TO GROW

Figs can be grown as freestanding trees or be trained as fans. Mulch around the base with well-rotted manure and keep plants well-watered, particularly in summer. Apply a high-potash fertilizer every couple of weeks in the growing season, until the figs begin to ripen. Prune in spring, wearing gloves to protect skin from irritating sap.

UNEXPECTED FLOWER
Figs are not really fruit but, in fact, flowers blooming and setting seed within a syconium – the hollow fleshy structure we call the fruit.

GROWING TIP

Plants can produce fruit twice a year, in spring and in summer, and this means that there will be fruit of different sizes by the end of summer. The largest will soon ripen and can be picked, and the very smallest will ripen next year so can be left. However, the medium-sized fruit should be removed.

NOTABLE CULTIVARS

- 'BrownTurkey' is a reliable variety for cool-temperate areas.
- 'Brunswick' bears purple-flushed, pear-shaped fruit.
- 'Chicago Hardy' is early fruiting, with deep mahogany figs.
- 'Petite Nigra' is good for containers and has small, dark fruit.
- 'Rouge de Bordeaux' needs a greenhouse or sheltered wall in cool-temperate areas.
- 'Violette Dauphine' has delicious, purple figs; train against a sunny wall if grown outdoors.
- 'White Marseilles' bears delicious, sweet, pale green fruit.

Planting a fig

With their pretty, hand-shaped leaves, crinkly bark and spreading habit, figs are lovely-looking trees with the bonus that they produce delicious fruit at the end of summer.

They have a reputation for being difficult to cultivate, and they do need a warm, sheltered, sunny spot. They are also very particular about how they are grown and like to have their roots restricted. If they are allowed to grow freely, their roots stretch out and the plant puts on lots of green growth but very little fruit. When the roots are contained, however, the fig tree will be smaller – about half the size it could reach – but it will fruit freely.

The easiest way to restrict fig roots is to grow the tree in a container around 50cm/20in in diameter. Water regularly – daily during dry weather in summer – and feed every two weeks with a high-potash fertilizer in the growing season. The top few centimetres of compost also needs refreshing every spring. Every three or four years repot your fig into a slightly larger container – no earlier as they fruit best when slightly pot-bound.

Alternatively, you can restrict fig roots in the open ground. Root-control bags are available; these are made of a special mesh fabric that prevents roots growing through it; or you can create a open-bottomed box within the ground using vertical paving slabs. Do not worry too much about getting the slabs neat and tight against each other – some constriction is enough. Just give the fig enough room to get established in the ground first before the roots nudge the slab.

Move figs grown in pots indoors over winter or insulate them with straw or dry leaves, secured with bubble wrap or horticultural fleece, to protect them through the cold winter months.

1. Figs grow very happily in pots 50–60cm/20–24in in diameter. Keeping them slightly pot-bound will increase yields, so repot only every three or four years.
2. Creating a box in the ground around the root ball helps contain a fig's roots. Paving slabs sunk into a pit work well.
3. At the end of summer there may be a few differently sized fruit on your fig tree simultaneously. The largest should be almost ready to pick, and the very smallest will grow into next year's harvest. Nip off those that are sized in between.
4. After leaf fall, pack around a fig with straw or dry leaves and then wrap in horticultural fleece. Remove the wrapping in late spring.

Apple

Malus domestica

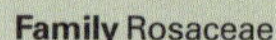

Family Rosaceae

Height and spread Depends on variety, rootstock and training

Hardiness Zone 6

Position Sunny and sheltered

Harvest Late summer–autumn

Being one of the most popular and widely cultivated tree fruits, there are a staggering 7,500 different varieties of apples. The apples we grow today have been grafted on to rootstocks to control their size and been bred for different tastes and uses – there are dessert and culinary varieties to choose from, as well as apples that are ideal for both uses. Apple trees are easy to grow and, although comparatively slow to crop, they will reward your patience with crisp, sweet fruit for years to come.

—

WHERE TO GROW

Apples are happiest in well-drained, fertile soil and a sunny, sheltered spot, but there are varieties to suit most soil types and situations. They tolerate winter temperatures down to –20°C/–4°F but not waterlogged ground. Apples grafted on to M9 dwarf rootstocks grow very well in containers.

HEALTH BENEFITS

Planting apples with garlic or near a walnut tree can help them to avoid apple scab – a fungal disease that causes dark, scabby marks on the fruit and leaves. A symbiotic relationship between the scab spores and the garlic or walnut keeps the trees scab free.

HOW TO GROW

Train as standards, bushes, spindles, pyramids, cordons, espaliers or fans (see Restricted tree forms, page 28). Unless you choose a self-fertile variety, you need to grow more than one apple variety and ensure they are both flowering at or around the same time so that pollination occurs and so fruit can develop (see also Pollination, page 13).

Trees are grouped according to when they flower, and apples from the same or adjoining pollination group need to be grown together. Ask for advice at your nursery as to which group the apple of your choice falls into. Then check which rootstock you need for the site in your garden where you want to grow your

apple tree. The most popular are: M27, M9, M26, MM106, MM111 or M25 (see Rootstocks, page 14).

If you have space for only one tree, check there are compatible trees in neighbouring parks or gardens, or opt for a family apple tree (see page 62). With two or more varieties grafted on to the trunk each main branch has a different apple, making a family tree a great choice for a small garden.

Give trees a boost with a sprinkle of general-purpose feed in spring. Water them in a dry summer and as the fruit starts to swell. Apples naturally drop excess fruit in early summer, often referred to as the 'June drop'. However, you may also have to thin out fruit yourself in midsummer, by taking away the 'king' apple at the centre of each cluster, to ensure the remaining apples ripen fully and to

stop the branches snapping under the weight of too much fruit.

Fruit is ready to harvest from late summer to autumn, depending on the variety. Windfalls on the ground are a good sign that fruit is ripe – the apples should come away from the tree with ease, when gently lifted.

Early types of apple should be eaten straight away, as they do not last for long, but other varieties frequently require a short period of storage until they are ready to eat. Many can be stored for up to six months in a cool, dark, frost-free place.

NOTABLE CULINARY CULTIVARS

- 'Annie Elizabeth' (Group 4) has exceptionally sweet flavour; keeps well.
- 'Arthur Turner' (Group 3) has beautiful blossom; fruit cooks down to a sweet, yellow purée.
- 'Bramley's Seedling' (Group 3) is a vigorous tree for the big garden; the apples make a creamy purée when cooked.
- 'Howgate Wonder' (Group 4) bears large fruit that hold its shape well when cooked; also makes lovely juice.
- 'Reverend W. Wilks' (Group 2) is a small, compact variety, with huge fruit that melts to a light, sweet purée.

NOTABLE DESSERT CULTIVARS

- 'Discovery' (Group 3) is an early fruiter with good disease resistance; the flesh is firm, sweet and juicy
- 'Egremont Russet' (Group 2) bears small, golden fruit with a rough skin and patches of russetting; the flavour has a hint of honey and nuts.
- 'Fiesta' (Group 3) is reliable, heavy cropping and has fine-flavoured, orange-flushed fruit.
- 'Greensleaves' (Group 3) bears light, crispy and crunchy, pale yellow fruit; leave to mellow on the tree before picking.
- 'Pixie' (Group 4) produces small, juicy, yellow fruit flushed with red; is good for a container.
- 'Spartan' (Group 3) has very juicy, deep plum-red fruit with white flesh; stays late on the tree and stores well.

NOTABLE DUAL-PURPOSE CULTIVARS

- 'Blenheim Orange' (Group 3) is vigorous, requires a dwarfing rootstock and crops heavily with sweet, firm fruit.
- 'Veitch's Perfection' (Group 4) bears sweet, sharp, nutty-flavoured fruit with a firm texture.

GROWING TIP

Pruning depends on how the tree has been trained and where it bears fruit – apples are either tip- or spur-bearing. Most apples are spur-bearing, which means they produce fruit in clusters on stubby, little branches (or spurs). These need pruning in winter by reducing laterals back by a third and sublaterals back to five buds to promote the growth of more fruiting buds.

Tip-bearing trees produce fruit on the tips of last year's growth. These trees are pruned in winter by taking out a quarter of the oldest wood every four years.

Summer pruning is mainly for trees that are trained as restricted forms such as fans, espaliers and cordons (see Restricted tree forms, page 28). New shoots are shortened so that light and air can reach the developing fruit.

Family apple trees

When space is limited, a family tree is a great way to grow more than one variety of tree fruit. One, two, three, even four different varieties are grafted on to the same stem, to create an entire orchard on a single tree; thus a family tree comprises a small central stem with an arm for each variety radiating from it. The varieties are selected to have compatible flowering times so they cross-pollinate each other to ensure fruit set (see Pollination, page 13). They are also usually chosen to ripen at slightly different times, to extend the harvest and make sure that there is not a glut of apples all at once.

Generally grown on a semi-dwarfing rootstocks (see Rootstocks, page 14), family trees are ideal for growing in large containers as well as in the ground. Be sure to place your pot in its final, sheltered, sunny spot before planting up, because it will be heavy to move once full of compost and your new tree. Make sure the tree is planted at the same depth it was before, by checking the soil mark on the stem. Stake your tree after planting, as it may struggle to support the fruit crop. Do this by inserting a stake at a 45-degree angle to the trunk, to which it is then tied. For planting family apple trees in the open ground, see page 25.

Trees grown in a pot need careful watering, particularly during dry periods in the growing season. Once blossom appears, feed each week with a high-potash liquid feed. As the tree grows, pot it up into a slightly larger pot each spring for the first three or four years.

Family trees can be trickier to prune than other trees as the different varieties often grow at different rates, and more care will be needed to keep them balanced and not lopsided.

1. A family apple tree is a great way to grow more than one variety in a small space. When grown on the appropriate rootstock, it is also perfectly happy in a pot.
2. Place soil-based potting compost in the base of the pot, then set the tree on top to check it is the correct depth. If the roots are too long for the pot, trim them with secateurs.
3. Place the tree in the pot again, making sure it is at the same depth as it was in its original pot or that the graft union is level with the rim if planting a bare-root tree.
4. Water the tree in well. It needs careful watering in its first year, to ensure it establishes successfully.
5. Mulching the surface of the compost with gravel or small stones helps to hold in moisture and reduces the need for constant watering.

1

2

3

4

5

Medlar

Mespilus germanica aka common medlar

One of the few fruits that are ripe in winter are medlars, which have a unique rich, musky taste, somewhere between a date and a spiced apple sauce. They require bletting before they are edible – a process of softening that makes the fruit sweeter – and have been eaten since Roman times.

–

Family Rosaceae

Height and spread 6 x 8m/20 x 26ft

Hardiness Zone 6

Position Sunny and open

Harvest Mid-autumn

WHERE TO GROW

Although happiest in an open, sunny site, medlars tolerate dappled shade but expect flowering, fruiting and their bright autumn leaf colour to be reduced. Avoid frost pockets as these trees flower in late spring.

HOW TO GROW

Use a Quince A rootstock. Trees are self-fertile and extremely undemanding. They tend to spread, so prune if needed in winter.

GROWING TIP

Harvest after the first hard frost, which helps to speed up the softening process by breaking down the cell walls. Blet the fruits by storing them somewhere cool and dark for a few weeks until they are ripe.

RECENT REVELATION
Mespilus germanica was the only known species of medlar until 1990, when a new species, *M. canescens*, was found in a small wood in Arkansas, USA.

NOTABLE CULTIVARS

- 'Dutch' is a vigorous spreading tree bearing large fruit.
- 'Flanders Giant' has very large fruit.
- 'Nottingham' is compact and reliable, with fruit even on young trees.
- 'Royal' bears late-ripening fruit on small trees.

Mulberry

Morus nigra aka black mulberry

Mulberries are spreading, self-fertile trees that become beautifully gnarled as they age, and they produce rich, tart and juicy fruit that is rarely available to buy in the shops. Trees can take up to ten years to fruit, so look for earlier fruiting varieties (see box, right).

–

Family Moraceae

Height and spread 9 x 9m/30 x 30ft

Hardiness Zone 6

Position Sunny and sheltered

Harvest Late summer

WHERE TO GROW

Mulberries thrive in deep, moisture-retentive but well-drained soil with a pH of 6–7. Plant them against a warm, sunny wall in cold, exposed gardens.

HOW TO GROW

Plant in spring as the soil warms up. Mulch in spring and water well through dry spells as the fruit develops. Prune trees, if necessary, in late autumn or winter, when fully dormant.

GROWING TIP

Harvest fruit by shaking the mulberries on to a sheet spread beneath the canopy. Wear gloves to collect them to prevent your hands from staining.

NOTABLE CULTIVARS

- 'Carman' has large, creamy white fruit; trees start to fruit at three or four years old, and also crop early in summer.
- 'Chelsea' fruits are large and richly sweet.
- 'Illinois Everbearing' has intensely sweet, black fruit cropping from year three.
- 'Wellington' bears masses of well-flavoured fruit.

FOOD FOR SILK

The leaves of white mulberry (*Morus alba*) are the preferred food source of the silk moth (*Bombyx mori*), whose cocoons are used to make silk.

Myrtle

Myrtis communis aka common myrtle

With their shiny, pointed leaves and fluffy, fragrant, summer flowers, these self-fertile, evergreen shrubs are often grown as ornamental plants. The rounded, purple-black berries are sweet with a hint of juniper and rosemary, and they are delicious in desserts and liqueurs. Dried berries can also be crushed and used like pepper.

–

Family Myrtaceae

Height and spread 3 x 2m/10 x 7ft

Hardiness Zone 4

Position Warm, sunny and sheltered

Harvest Autumn

WHERE TO GROW

Happiest in a sunny border or tucked against a warm wall, myrtle still needs protection from drying winds. It grows well in a pot; move into a warmer spot in winter if needed. Myrtle needs fertile, moist but well-drained soil.

RICH BOUNTY

Myrtle offers double value – as well as the fruit, its fragrant leaves are lovely when crushed and used to flavour stews, roast meats and salad.

HOW TO GROW

Plant in spring in the ground or in a pot. Water in the growing season. Mulch around the bases of plants with well-rotted garden compost or manure in early spring. Feed plants in pots with a high-potash feed in the growing season. Prune any unwanted growth in spring. In cool-temperate areas, protect plants against the winter wet and from cold, drying winds with horticultural fleece.

GROWING TIP

Myrtle berries need a long, hot summer to ripen, so in cool-temperate climates be sure to give plants your warmest, sunniest spot.

NOTABLE CULTIVAR

- 'Variegata' has silver-green leaves and pink-tinged flowers.

Olive

Olea europaea aka European olive

These beautiful, self-fertile, evergreen trees are native to the Mediterranean, and the fruit is used for oil and to eat.

–

WHERE TO GROW

Olives need well-drained soil. In cool-temperate regions, grow trees in pots and bring indoors over winter.

HOW TO GROW

Keep moist in the growing season and feed once a month with a balanced liquid fertilizer. Re-shape trees in spring.

GROWING TIP

Olives can be harvested when green (but then must be soaked in water before they are edible) or when black. Dry-cure black olives in salt to dehydrate them and then store in oil.

Family Oleaceae

Height and spread 10 x 10m/33 x 33ft

Hardiness Zone 4

Position Warm, sunny and sheltered

Harvest Autumn

LONGEVITY PAR EXCELLENCE

A number of olive trees in the Mediterranean area are believed to be as old as 2,000 years, but their average lifespan is 300–600 years.

NOTABLE CULTIVARS

- 'Arbequina' is a weeping form, with delicious, black olives.
- 'Frantoio' has fruity, aromatic oil.
- 'Leccino' is easy-to-grow and tolerant of a wide range of conditions.
- 'Lucca' produces masses of olives.
- 'Manzanillo' is the most widely grown olive variety in the world.

Apricot

Prunus armeniaca aka ansu apricot, Siberian apricot, Tibetan apricot, abricock

Delicately flavoured, sweetly aromatic apricots are delicious when eaten fresh. Dry or preserve the fruits of these self-fertile trees if you cannot eat them at once.

–

Family Rosaceae

Height and spread 3–5 x 4m/10–16 x 13ft

Hardiness Zone 6

Position Warm, sunny and sheltered

Harvest Midsummer–early autumn

WHERE TO GROW

Apricots like deep, fertile, well-drained soil, with plenty of well-rotted organic manure added in. They flower very early so avoid frost pockets.

HOW TO GROW

Train as a fan on a warm, sunny wall or grow as a freestanding tree. The most popular rootstock is St Julien A. Prune when the sap is rising in spring or summer; always protect flowers from frost, with fleece. Water well in the first few years.

GROWING TIP

Boost yields by hand-pollinating the flowers with a small, soft brush, because few pollinators are around when apricots are in bloom. Alternatively, look for later-flowering varieties.

POPULAR FOOD

Apricots have been cultivated for thousands of years and are rumoured to have been grown in India in 3000 BC. Despite their species name of *armeniaca*, they are thought to originate from China.

NOTABLE CULTIVARS

- 'Alfred' has medium-sized, pink-flushed, orange fruits.
- 'Garden Aprigold' is compact (to only 1.5m/5ft) and is ideal for containers; it has golden yellow fruit.
- 'Isabella' is compact and ideal for containers.
- 'Moorpark' is late cropping, with orange-red fruits.
- 'Tomcot' is early cropping, with red-flushed, orange fruits.

Cherry

Prunus avium aka sweet cherry
P. cerasus aka acid cherry, sour cherry

Like many other fruit trees, cherries are grouped according to when they flower, and older tree varieties that are not self-fertile must be grown with a compatible variety that flowers around the same time. Self-fertile and dwarfing varieties are readily available so the smallest garden, even a balcony, can have one. These are beautiful trees for the garden with spring blossom, delicious fruit and vivid autumn leaf colour. Cherries can be sweet or sour, and eaten fresh or cooked in jams and pies.

–

Family Rosaceae

Height and spread 3–8 x 1.5–4m/10–26 x 5–13ft

Hardiness Zone 6

Position (Sweet) Full sun and sheltered; (Sour) Shady and sheltered

Harvest Midsummer–early autumn

WHERE TO GROW

Cherries require good drainage. Sweet cherries need sun to ripen, while sour varieties thrive against a cool, shady wall.

HOW TO GROW

Cherries can be grown as freestanding trees or fans on Colt or Gisela 5 rootstocks. Mulch with organic matter in spring, and protect early blossom from frosts, with fleece. Keep trees well-watered when fruit sets, and net cherries to protect against birds as soon as they start to swell.

GROWING TIP

Prune cherries after harvesting, when the flow of sap will seal wounds; this helps to prevent silver leaf and canker. Sweet cherries fruit on older wood, so prune out some of the oldest wood to create a balance of old and new wood; also shorten new shoots in summer to encourage fruiting spurs.

Sour cherries fruit on the previous season's growth. Remove whole shoots in summer to reduce overcrowding and stimulate new growth.

SEIZE THE MOMENT
In Japanese culture, cherry blossom symbolizes impermanence and is seen as a reminder to celebrate life, knowing that it will not last.

NOTABLE CULTIVARS

Sweet

- 'Lapins' (self-fertile) bears lots of dark red cherries.
- 'Stella' (self-fertile) has large, black fruit.
- 'Summer Sun' (self-fertile) is suitable for a cool-temperate climate.

Sour

- 'Montmorency' (self-fertile) is believed to be the best for pies, with its rich, tangy fruits.
- 'Morello' (self-fertile) bears large, dark fruit, which is good in pies.
- 'Nabella' (self-fertile) is compact and heavy cropping, with bright red fruit.

Plum

Prunus domestica aka European plum

Plums are in a large group of stone fruits that also includes damsons (see page 73) and gages (see page 72). They are generally ovoid in shape and are dessert, culinary or dual-purpose. Although self-fertile varieties are available, such trees produce a bigger crop if more than one is planted in the vicinity. Plums are excellent when baked in crumbles and pies, while dessert ones are delicious when eaten fresh.

Family Rosaceae

Height and spread Depends on the rootstock

Hardiness Zone 6

Position Sunny and sheltered

Harvest Midsummer–mid-autumn

WHERE TO GROW

Plums like well-drained, fertile, heavy soil so add bulky organic matter to sandy ground to help it retain water. Avoid frost pockets and windy sites.

HOW TO GROW

Grow as a bush shape or train as a fan, cordon or minaret (see Restricted tree forms, page 28), on VVA1, Pixy or St Julien A rootstock. Blossom is susceptible to frost, so protect with fleece. Water well in the first few years.

GROWING TIP

Thin fruit in early summer, after the tree has naturally dropped its excess young fruit, in the 'June drop' (see Apple, page 57). If branches become too laden with fruit they may break under the weight, leaving the tree vulnerable to silver leaf or bacterial canker unless pruned in spring or summer.

WAXY COVER

Ripe plums have a dusty, white coating, or 'bloom', that gives them a glaucous appearance and protects them from drying out.

NOTABLE CULTIVARS

- 'Czar' (culinary) bears lots of dark purple plums.
- 'Marjorie's Seedling' (dual-purpose) is late-fruiting and so misses early frosts.
- 'Opal' (dessert) is a reliable variety, with red fruit.
- 'Victoria' (dessert) has delicious, yellow flesh.

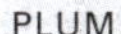

Gage

Prunus domestica

Gages can be yellow, purple or orange as well as green – and come in dessert, culinary or dual-purpose types. Self-fertile varieties are available, but trees produce a bigger crop if more than one is planted.

Family Rosaceae

Height and spread Depends on the rootstock

Hardiness Zone 6

Position Sunny and sheltered

Harvest Midsummer–mid-autumn

—

WHERE TO GROW

Grow in fertile, well-drained soil and protect from harsh winds and frost. Early blossom is susceptible to damage from late frosts.

HOW TO GROW

Use VVA1, Pixy or St Julien A rootstocks. The fruits should be at their most delicious and juicy when trees are fan-trained against a warm, sunny wall. Buy part-trained trees and prune only in spring or summer to avoid silver leaf. Mulch in spring to reduce water loss, and thin fruit in summer after the natural 'June drop' (see Apple, page 57).

GROWING TIP

Wait until the skin around the stalk becomes slightly shrivelled before picking. Do not be tempted to harvest the fruit too early.

FRENCH ORIGINS

The small, green plums (gages) that were brought to the UK from France more than 300 years ago are all varieties of *Prunus domestica* but are more spherical than a traditional plum.

NOTABLE CULTIVARS

- 'Cambridge Gage' (partially self-fertile) is compact, with delicious, dessert fruit; needs another variety nearby.
- 'GoldenTransparent' (self-fertile) is reliable, with lots of deliciously sweet, yellow dessert fruit.
- 'Jefferson' (infertile) is a mid- to late-season, delicious, yellow dessert gage with some disease resistance; needs another variety growing nearby.
- 'Old Green Gage' (partially self-fertile) bears juicy, sweet, yellow culinary gages.
- 'Oullins Gage' (self-fertile) bears lots of fine-flavoured, dual-purpose, golden fruit; is a good pollinator for other trees.

Damson

Prunus insititia aka damson plum, damascene

Undemanding trees, damsons are harder and smaller than other 'plums' and develop a tart skin that makes them excellent for cooking, jamming or making into liqueurs (see Making damson gin, page 74) rather than eating fresh from the tree. Even if you buy a self-fertile variety, it will produce a bigger crop if you have more than one damson tree nearby.

–

Family Rosaceae

Height and spread 3 x 3m/10 x 10ft

Hardiness Zone 6

Position Sunny and sheltered

Harvest Late summer–early autumn

WHERE TO GROW

Damson trees survive in all but waterlogged and chalky ground. Protect the blossom against frost while ensuring pollinating insects can access the flowers.

HOW TO GROW

Choose VVA1, Pixy or St Julien A rootstock. Mulch with well-rotted manure in mid-spring. Always prune in spring or summer, to avoid infection from bacterial canker and silver leaf.

GROWING TIP

Boost fruit size, ease congestion in the tree canopy and avoid snapping branches by thinning fruit in midsummer, after the tree's natural 'June drop' (see Apple, page 57).

NOTABLE CULTIVARS

- 'Bradley's King Damson' has large, very sweet, radiant purple fruit.
- 'Farleigh Damson' is late cropping, with lots of delicious, purple fruit.
- 'Merryweather Damson' is easy and reliable, with fruit that can be eaten raw or cooked.
- 'Prune Damson' is a mid-season variety, with astringent fruit that becomes intensely flavoured once cooked.

BROUGHT BY IMMIGRANTS

English settlers introduced damsons to the American colonies in the mid-eighteenth century, before the American Revolution, where they thrived better than other plum species.

Making damson gin

Preserving the essence of fruit by steeping it in alcohol has been a favourite way of enjoying a taste of summer or autumn long after these seasons have passed. Hedgerow berries such as sloes (*Prunus spinosa*) are a traditional choice, but lots of home-grown fruit works deliciously well too. Damsons or plums are tangy and rich in flavour, or you could try cherries or berries such as raspberries, blueberries, blackberries and currants. There is no reason why you could not use gin or vodka, even brandy, for the base of your drink. Different fruits do seem to suit certain alcohol so it is worth experimenting. It takes two to three months to infuse the fruit and for the flavour to mature, getting smoother and better with time.

Traditionally, fruit is collected only after the first frost, but you can simulate this in the freezer, where the cold chill helps to split the skin, open the fruit cells and get the juices flowing. Before placing the fruit in the freezer overnight, rinse it and pat it dry.

The next day put the frozen fruit into a clean jar or bottle, filling it about halfway. Add a couple of tablespoons of sugar and then top up with your alcohol of choice. Put the lid on securely, give the container a good shake to mix everything together and then store it in a cupboard. Shake it daily for the next week, to stop the sugar settling on the bottom and to help the fruit release its juice. Thereafter, the container needs shaking just once a week for the next couple of months. Then taste the liquid: once the fruit has instilled its flavour, strain the liquid into another clean bottle. It is now ready to be enjoyed.

Some people believe that the use of cheap alcohol results in an inferior tasting liqueur; others, that the flavour of the fruit is so overpowering that this does not matter. However, the longer you leave the mix to steep, the smoother it will be, so if you can afford only cheap alcohol leave the mix for as long as you can.

1. Harvest your damsons when they are ripe – the first few fruits dropping from the tree are a good sign. They should also come away easily when you pick them.
2. Freezing the fruit helps to split the skin, making it easier for it to release its juice and infuse the alcohol.
3. Use a sterilized jar or bottle that can be sealed, add the fruit and sugar, and then top up with the gin. Give the container a good shake.
4. When it is ready, use a funnel to filter the liqueur and decant it into a clean, dry bottle, then seal it.
5. Label the bottle, and it is ready to drink. The liqueur will keep for more than a year – if you can last that long.

Peach and nectarine

Prunus persica, P. persica var. *nectarina*

A soft, juicy peach – evocative of Mediterranean holidays and warm, sunny days – and its smoother-skinned 'cousin' the nectarine are surprisingly easy to grow, even in cool-temperate climates. They just need a warm, bright spot and sufficient time to ripen in the sun.

–

WHERE TO GROW

Give these self-fertile trees a sheltered home such as a warm, sunny wall to protect the early spring blossom from frost, the leaves from rain and peach leaf curl and to ensure that the fruit ripens. Grow in a fertile, well-drained soil. When grown in a greenhouse, they require careful watering.

HOW TO GROW

Choose VVA1 or St Julien A rootstock and grow as a fan against a warm wall. (You can buy two- or three-year-old plants ready trained as fans.) Peaches can also be grown as small, freestanding trees, but nectarines struggle in such a form. Compact forms of both fruits grow happily in pots.

Peaches and nectarines fruit on the previous season's wood so need replacement pruning in spring or summer, to produce a supply of new wood and to avoid silver leaf disease.

Mulch plants with organic matter in spring. Hand-pollinate their early blossom with a soft brush throughout the flowering season. Also, protect the flowers from early spring frosts.

Family Rosaceae

Height and spread 2.5–4 x 2.5–4m/ 8–13 x 8–13ft

Hardiness Zone 4

Position Warm, sunny and sheltered

Harvest Midsummer–early autumn

GEOGRAPHIC POINTER

The specific name *persica* is a reference to the peach's widespread cultivation in Persia, now Iran, from where it was then introduced into Europe.

As the fruit starts to swell, water well. Ripe fruit should come away easily from the tree.

GROWING TIP

As the fruits develop, thin them to 10cm/4in apart, to allow the remaining fruits to reach their full size – and obtain their maximum sugar levels.

NOTABLE CULTIVARS

Peach

- 'Bonanza' is a dwarf tree that is perfect for container growing, reaching just 1.5m/5ft tall after ten years; it is heavy cropping with yellow-fleshed fruit.
- 'Duke of York' is early fruiting, with juicy, white flesh and a crimson skin.
- 'Garden Lady' bears pink blossom and yellow-fleshed, freestone fruit; is compact, less than 2m/7ft high, and suitable for containers.
- 'Peregrine' is an old variety, with delicious, green-and-crimson-skinned, white-fleshed fruit.
- 'Rochester' produces large, juicy, yellow-fleshed fruit; as it is a freestone variety, the flesh comes away easily from the stone.

Nectarine

- 'John Rivers' is early ripening, with large, golden yellow fruit and a rich, sweet flavour.
- 'Lord Napier' produces heavy crops of juicy, tasty, crimson-and-pale-yellow fruit in late summer.
- 'Nectarella' is a dwarf variety for growing in pots; although slow-growing it often crops within the first or second year.
- 'Pineapple' is greeny-red-skinned with golden flesh that melts in the mouth and has a hint of pineapple.

Pomegranate

Punica granatum

Fast-growing, frost-hardy pomegranate shrubs or trees thrive in hot, dry conditions and are self-fertile. They take just 2–3 years to fruit, producing bright scarlet flowers followed by their distinctive, rounded fruits.

–

Family Lythraceae

Height and spread 3 x 2m/10 x 7ft

Hardiness Zone 3

Position Full sun

Harvest Late summer–autumn

WHERE TO GROW

Pomegranates fruit best on deep, heavy, well-drained soil in full sun. In cold regions (Zone 4 and below), grow plants in pots and move them under cover as soon as temperatures start to drop in winter.

HOW TO GROW

Prune in spring and summer, and give plants a high-potash liquid feed in summer to promote a heavy crop. In the wild, pomegranates grow as multi-stemmed shrubs and can be cultivated as such in the garden or else pruned into a single-stemmed tree.

GROWING TIP

Harvest fruit before it cracks open on the plant. Try tapping the fruit; if you hear a metallic sound, it is ready to be cut.

NOTABLE CULTIVARS

- 'Ambrosia' produces very large, pale pink fruits with a tangy, sweet juice.
- 'Fleishman' bears large, rounded, pink fruits with pink flesh and very soft seeds.
- 'Kashmir' bears intensely flavoured, deep red fruits.
- 'Parfianka' is an upright tree, with bright red, sweet, slightly acidic fruit.

FAMED FOR FECUNDITY

Cultivated since ancient times, pomegranates symbolize fertility in many cultures from China to India.

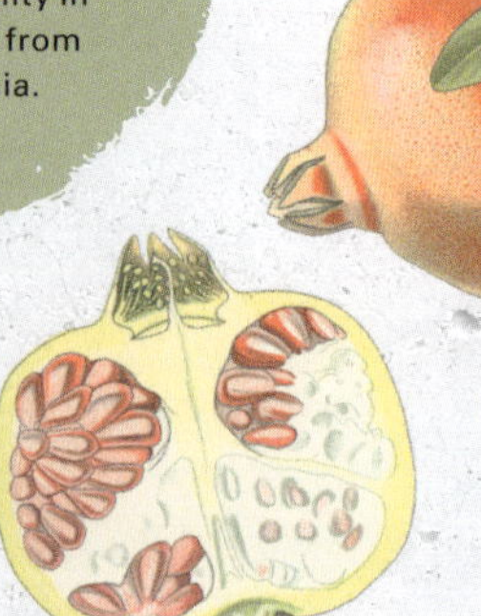

Pear

Pyrus communis

Home-grown pears are a succulent tree fruit with a depth of flavour and a sweet juiciness that is unlike anything you can buy in shops. Unlike apples, pears cannot be eaten fresh from the tree; instead, they are picked early and brought in, to ripen indoors, brilliantly avoiding any pests and diseases that can occur prior to harvesting. Self-fertile varieties are available but all pears do better when grown with others from the same pollinating group.

—

WHERE TO GROW

Pears are easy trees to grow but do need to be kept away from frost pockets. Give them fertile, well-drained soil – they do not grow well on thin, shallow ones. They can also be grown in large containers, 40–50cm/16–20in across, provided they are grafted on to the dwarf container rootstock Quince C.

HOW TO GROW

Grow as freestanding trees or train as cordons, espaliers and fans (see Restricted tree forms, page 28). Pears are generally grafted on to Quince A or C rootstocks, and the correct one must be chosen for the type or size of pear you wish to grow.

Flowers need pollen from another tree to crop well (see Pollination, page 13). Pear cultivars are, therefore, grouped into four pollinating groups according to when they flower. To ensure a successful crop, grow cultivars from the same pollinating group. Also, protect blossom against frost with fleece, or grow a late-flowering cultivar. Feed in spring with a general fertilizer.

The natural 'June drop' in early summer (see Apple, page 57) may not be enough to allow fruit to ripen fully and to prevent

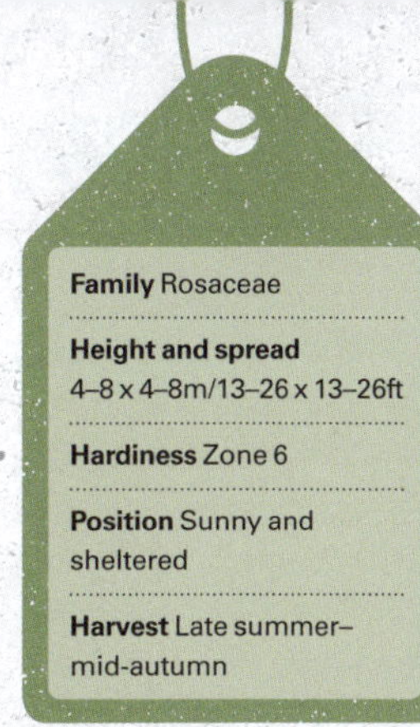

Family Rosaceae

Height and spread 4–8 x 4–8m/13–26 x 13–26ft

Hardiness Zone 6

Position Sunny and sheltered

Harvest Late summer–mid-autumn

CHARACTERISTIC STRUCTURE

The distinctive, fine, gritty texture of pear flesh is formed by clusters of stone cells. Also known as scleroids, they are found in other hard tissues such as peach stones and walnut shells.

branches breaking under the weight of the fruit, so remove all but two pears per cluster in midsummer. Water trees in dry summers and as soon as the fruit starts to swell.

Harvest pears just before they are fully ripe – look for windfalls on the ground and a subtle flushing of the skin. They should also be easy to pick, coming away with the stalk intact. Store in a cool, dark place to mature. Fruit can also be dried and it will last for up to six months (see Perfectly preserved dried fruit, page 82).

GROWING TIP

Prune freestanding trees or bushes in winter, by reducing the branch leaders by a third, to promote fruiting spurs. Restricted forms such as cordons, espaliers, stepovers and fans are pruned predominantly in late summer, with the side branches reduced to three leaves. Thin the fruiting stems to 10cm/4in apart in winter.

NOTABLE CULTIVARS

- 'Beth' (Group 4) is an upright variety, with small, sweet, pale yellow pears.
- 'Beurré d'Anjou' (Group 3) is a heritage variety, with delicious, juicy, white flesh.
- 'Beurré Hardy' (Group 3) needs a sheltered spot to produce its reddish-green fruit.
- 'Concorde' (Group 4) is compact, with good yields of sweet, juicy fruit.
- 'Conference' (Group 3) is easy to grow and heavy cropping, with a distinctive shape and good flavour.
- 'Doyenné du Comice' (Group 4) bears utterly delicious fruit with a sweet aroma; needs plenty of warmth.
- 'Fondante d'Automne' (Group 3) has musky flesh and a russet skin.
- 'Glou Morceau' (Group 4) is a late-fruiting, with a delicate flavour and buttery flesh.
- Invincible ('Delwinor') (Group 2) has sweet, juicy fruit that stores well.
- 'Onward' (Group 4) bears reliable, juicy fruit that needs to be eaten straight away.
- 'Williams' Bon Chrétien' (Group 3) has good flavour and is easy to grow.

Perfectly preserved dried fruit

Drying removes the water content from fruit, shrinking it and creating an delicious, energy-dense snack that lasts much longer than fresh fruit. Dried fruit is not only additive-free but also full of fibre and nutrients and is a really easy way to get your 'five a day'. It also looks beautiful and makes gorgeous natural decorations perfect for the holiday season or for use year-round.

Fruit drying can be done naturally, in the sun or in a low-temperature oven or specialized dehydrator. Dehydrators are efficient and easy to use, but are an investment and probably worth buying only if you definitely plan to do a lot of fruit drying. They can be quite expensive and also take up space in the kitchen.

Apples dry really easily but all fruit can be dried, from citrus and apricots to kiwi fruit, strawberries, figs and plums. Those that are particularly water-dense, such as apricots and grapes, take longer than others to process.

Wash fruit well and then soak for a few minutes before slicing thinly and evenly so that all the pieces will dry at the same rate. Then lay the slices out, without overlapping, on racks for the oven or the dehydrator. Dehydrators will have specific temperatures and timings for individual fruit, while using the oven is a little more variable. Set the oven at its lowest setting and keep checking on your fruit. Fan ovens will dry the fruit slices quicker than other types of oven, but all will take hours rather than minutes. Once you know how long the process takes, why not dry fruit overnight to save time?

When your dried fruit slices have cooled, they can be stored in an airtight container for up to six months or be used to make beautiful natural decorations and ornaments.

1 Finely slice the fruit and lay each piece evenly on racks without overlapping. Place in a very low-temperature oven overnight.
2 Dehydrators are an easy and efficient way to dry fruit such as these pear slices, to make a tasty and nutrient-rich snack.
3 Dried apple slices can be dipped in chocolate to make tasty presents or be hung with ribbon as Christmas tree decorations.
4 When sliced so that each piece has the stem in the centre, fruits such as citrus, apples and kiwi fruit make a beautiful garland.
5 Slices of dried citrus fruit form a gorgeous wreath that can be hung throughout autumn and winter.

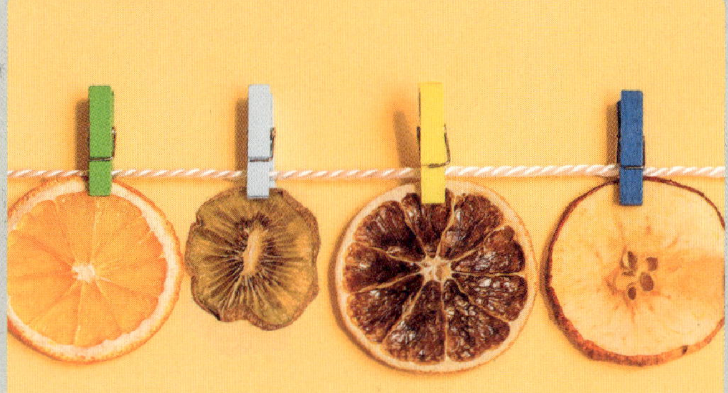

Soft fruit

Kiwi fruit

Actinidia deliciosa aka Chinese gooseberry, fuzzy kiwi fruit

Family Actinidaceae

Height and spread 6 x 4m/20 x 13ft

Hardiness Zone 4

Position Sunny and sheltered

Harvest Autumn

Being vigorous, these deciduous climbing plants demand space but reward you with an abundance of tasty, zingy fruit three or four years after planting. Decorative plants in their own right with velvety, heart-shaped leaves, they also have large, white flowers.

—

WHERE TO GROW

Kiwi fruit prefers well-drained, moisture-retentive soil. New shoots are vulnerable to frost damage so support the plant against a warm, sunny wall.

HOW TO GROW

Mulch with organic matter in late winter, and feed with a general fertilizer in spring. Protect plants against late frost with fleece in spring. Keep plants well-watered as the fruit start to swell and thin your crop, if necessary, for larger fruit. Prune in summer to keep plants in shape, within their allotted space. To promote fruiting growth, cut back side shoots to four or five leaves in winter.

GROWING TIP

Plants may be self-fertile, female or (non-fruiting) male. Self-fertile varieties set fruit when pollinated by insects, while female plants bear fruit only after pollination by flowers of a male variety, so male and female varieties are needed to ensure a crop.

NOTABLE CULTIVARS

- 'Atlas' (male) is vigorous and hardy; pollinates all female varieties.
- 'Hayward' (female) is the 'original' and popular variety developed in New Zealand in 1924.
- 'Jenny' (self-fertile) produces delicious, green-and-brown fruit.
- 'Monty' (female) is late-flowering, with oblong fruit.
- *Actinidia arguta* 'Ken's Red' (female) bears mild, sweet, red fruit.

MOVING ON

Native to China, where they are the national fruit, cultivation of what was called Chinese gooseberry spread to New Zealand in the early twentieth century and commercial planting began there in the 1940s. In 1959 it was renamed kiwi fruit after New Zealand's brown and furry national bird.

Melon and watermelon

Cucumis melo aka sweet melon, apple cucumber, cucumber vine; *Citrullus lanatus* aka watermelon

Melons (*Cucumis melo*) are tender, self-fertile annuals from the tropics that will scramble on the ground or climb up supports in a sunny spot. There are three main types: cantaloupe (usually with a ribbed skin and orange flesh), honeydew (yellow flesh) and musk (distinctive, netted skin and green or orange flesh). Cantaloupe melons cope best with cool-temperate weather, needing less heat and sun to ripen.

Watermelons (*Citrullus lanatus*) have a distinctive, striped skin and bright pink flesh.

–

WHERE TO GROW

In cool-temperate climates, grow melons in a greenhouse or against a sunny wall – melons grow successfully outside only in warmer climates. Plant in humus-rich, well-drained soil. Loosen the soil before planting so that roots can spread easily in search of water and nutrients.

Watermelons need lots of sunshine and water to ripen.

HOW TO GROW

Sow seeds of melons and watermelons in small pots indoors or in a propagator in spring (see Growing melons from seed, page 90). Young plants can also be bought and grown on later in the season. Keep plants moist and harden them off before planting outside once there is little risk of frosts. Just cover the root ball with soil; if planted too low, plants can rot.

Thereafter, keep plants well-watered. Put up netting or a framework for plants to scramble up, and pinch off the growing tips to encourage side shoots, which will produce

Family Cucurbitaceae

Height and spread 1.2 x 0.6m/4 x 2ft

Hardiness Zone 1

Position Hot, sunny and sheltered

Harvest Late summer–mid-autumn

NOTABLE CULTIVARS

Melon

- 'Blenheim Orange' (musk) has sweetly fragranced, scarlet flesh.
- 'Early Dawn' (musk) is high-yielding, with green-netted skin and orange flesh; early ripening.
- 'Emir' (musk) has sweetly fragrant, orange flesh; tolerates cool-temperate temperatures well.
- 'Fastbreak' (cantaloupe) is high-yielding, with deep salmon-coloured flesh; early cropping.
- 'Galia' (cantaloupe/honeydew cross) has golden skin and pale green flesh.
- 'Rugoso di Cosenza Giallo' (cantaloupe) has large, yellow fruit with sweet, juicy flesh.
- 'Sweetheart' (cantaloupe) is rounded with cream skin and orange flesh.

Watermelon

- 'Mini Love' is compact and early ripening, with sweet, red flesh.
- 'Sugar Baby' produces melons small enough to fit in the refrigerator; it has firm, red fruit.

JAPANESE TREASURE
'Yubari King' melon is a cross between two types of cantaloupe that is grown only in the Yūbari region of Japan. Reported to be the sweetest melons in the world, they are often given as gifts, and in 2017 two were sold at auction for three million yen.

the fruiting flowers. Ensure pollination in a greenhouse by ventilating when plants are in flower. Also shade plants grown under glass in summer, and give them a steady supply of water to avoid attack by red spider mite. Feed with a high-potash fertilizer or a comfrey feed every week, once the fruits are the size of walnuts. At the same time, snip off the growing tips, a couple of leaves beyond each fruit, to divert energy into the fruit. Stop watering and feeding once melons start to ripen. Support swelling melons in nets, cloth bags or old stockings.

A sweet, heady fragrance should alert you that the melons are ripe but fruit will also start to split and soften around the stem.

GROWING TIP
Hand-pollinate plants grown under glass by brushing pollen from the male to the female flowers, with a small, soft brush. A swelling behind the flower is a sign of a female flower.

Growing melons from seed

One of the few annual fruit plants that needs growing from scratch every year are melons. Each melon plant should produce between two and four melons. Young plants can be bought from the garden centre or online, but they are really easy-to-grow from seed, which is a much cheaper method, more rewarding and offers a far wider range of varieties.

Seeds can be sown in a greenhouse or on a sunny windowsill, from early spring, or directly outside from mid-spring. Sow the seed into modular trays, which have individual cells for single seeds, or into 9cm/3½cm pots, which can hold up to four seeds each. Use a specialized seed compost such as John Innes No. 1 or a finely sieved multipurpose potting compost. Lay seeds on their sides and then cover with a fine layer of sharp sand or more sieved compost. Keep the plants warm (at a minimum 15–20°C/ 59–68°F) and the compost moist; germination should take about a week. Once three or four leaves have formed, the seedlings can be potted on and grown in a greenhouse or be planted outside in the garden in a warm, sunny spot from late spring. In cool-temperate climates, wait until there is little risk of frosts. Thereafter, refer to How to grow, page 88.

1

2

1 Fill a modular seed tray with potting compost, firm it down with your fingers and sow one seed per cell. Cover thinly.
2 Grow the seedlings on until they have three or four leaves. Then pot them on into individual pots.
3 In cool-temperate areas, melons are best grown in a greenhouse or polytunnel. Plant so the top of the root ball is just below the soil level, and space plants 60cm/24in apart.
4 As the fruit starts to swell it can get quite heavy; stop it from falling off the plant by supporting it with netting, old sacking or tights until it is ripe.
5 Melons are ripe when they start to release a strong, sweet scent. Cup the melon in your hand and cut it carefully from the plant.

3

4

5

Strawberry

Fragaria × ananassa aka garden strawberry

Deliciously sweet and aromatic strawberries are the taste of summer for many, and the flavour of home-grown ones surpasses that of any strawberries you would find in shops. They are very easy to grow and are produced on tiny, low-growing, self-fertile plants.

–

Family Rosaceae

Height and spread 30 x 45cm/12 x 18in

Hardiness Zone 6

Position Sunny and sheltered

Harvest Spring–autumn, depending on type

WHERE TO GROW

Strawberries are versatile plants that thrive in pots and baskets as well as in the ground. They prefer fertile, well-drained soil and are best kept out of windy sites and frost pockets. Avoid planting where any member of the Solanaceae family (potatoes, tomatoes, aubergines) has recently been growing as these plants are susceptible to verticillium wilt, which can kill strawberries.

HOW TO GROW

Plant young plants, or runners, in late summer or early autumn, with each crown level with the soil surface: if planted too high, it dries out; if too low, it can rot.

Water little and often because strawberries are shallow-rooting and can dry out quickly, but they also hate sitting in wet soil. Unless you wish to propagate new plants from runners (see page 94), remove these as soon as you spot them, to concentrate energy into flower and fruit production.

Once flowers appear, give plants a weekly high-potash liquid feed. Mulching plants with straw or strawberry mats helps to conserve

WELCOME MIXTURE

The strawberries we eat today are the result of a cross between *F. virginiana* from America and the Chilean *F. chiloensis* in the eighteenth century.

NOTABLE CULTIVARS

Early season

- 'Gariguette' bears sweetly flavoured, elongated fruit.
- 'Honeoye' has lots of sweet, deep red fruit.
- 'Mae' produces large, firm, juicy fruit.

Mid-season

- 'Cambridge Favourite' is reliable, with sweet, medium-sized fruit.
- 'Hapil' is good for relatively dry soil and has heavy yields.
- 'Royal Sovereign' is delicious and deeply aromatic.

Late-season

- 'Fenella' has lots of large, glossy fruit.
- 'Florence' bears dark, sweet fruit and has good disease resistance.
- 'Malwina' produces large, fragrant, deep red fruit.

Perpetuals

- 'Albion' produces very large, sweet, fragrant fruit from early summer to late autumn.
- 'Aromel' has lovely flavoured, medium-sized fruit.
- 'Flamenco' bears sweet, juicy fruit over a long picking period.

TYPES OF STRAWBERRIES

There are three main types of strawberry: summer bearers, which are grouped according to when they fruit in early, mid- or late summer; perpetuals, also called everbearers or remontant, which produce small flushes of fruit from midsummer to early autumn; and wild strawberries (see page 96).

moisture in the soil and keep fruit clean and dry. Plants may also need netting to protect fruit from the birds and squirrels.

After fruiting, cut off old leaves with a knife, taking care not to cut the crowns, then clear away any straw to expose the crowns to the winter cold to come. Water plants if very dry, to promote healthy new growth.

GROWING TIP

Strawberries can be grown under cover to extend the cropping season but this can make it difficult for pollinating insects to reach flowers. Help your plants by opening doors and vents on warm days, and hand-pollinate flowers with a small brush.

Propagating strawberries from runners

Strawberries are easy plants to grow and they are also very simple to propagate, which is handy as they fruit well for only three or four years and then need replacing.

Plants spread rapidly producing abundant runners – long stems growing out from the centre of the plant with baby plants on the end; each will root into the ground to grow into a new plant. Runners absorb a lot of energy from the strawberry plant that could be focused on producing flowers and fruit, so when propagation is not required always cut off the runners, taking them out from the base. However, once plants start to weaken in their third year, new plants can be encouraged – and they are, of course, free. Both strawberries growing in the ground and those in containers can be increased by runners.

Ideally, plants should be propagated when they have finished fruiting at the end of summer and no later than early autumn. Fill small pots with multipurpose potting compost and sink them into the ground next to the 'mother' plant, which helps to retain moisture, or else place each pot on the soil itself. Insert the runners into the compost in each pot and secure in place with a U-shaped staple or piece of bent wire.

Within 4–6 weeks the baby plants will have rooted and started to grow new leaves; they can then be cut free from the parent plant. Grow them on over winter, and pot on or plant out in the ground the following spring. Always plant new strawberry plants into a fresh spot in the garden, to prevent the build-up of disease. Nip out flowers in the first year, to encourage strong productive plants and prevent fruiting.

1. Most types of strawberry, apart from perpetual or everbearers, produce lots of runners. Perpetual types are best replaced every year rather than propagated.
2. Choose a healthy runner and place it on the surface of the pot of compost or soil, pinning it down with a thin piece of wire bent into a U shape. Do not snip off the stem linking the two plants.
3. Keep the compost or soil well-watered to help promote root growth.
4. Once each young plant has strongly rooted, separate it from its parent by cutting off the stem that links them together.
5. Grow the young plants on over winter and then plant out in spring into the ground or into larger pots.

1

2

3

4

5

Wild strawberry

Fragaria vesca aka alpine strawberry, woodland strawberry, Carpathian strawberry, fraisier des bois

Family Rosaceae

Height and spread 30 x 65cm/12 x 26in

Hardiness Zone 6

Position Sun or partial shade and sheltered

Harvest Late spring–autumn

Dainty, delicate fruit is produced in several flushes on low, spreading, self-fertile, bushy plants that grow happily in containers or in the ground. Despite their size, these are tough perennials and the ruby-red fruit has an intense flavour and fragrance.

–

WHERE TO GROW

Plants crop best in a sunny, sheltered spot and fertile, well-drained soil. In poor soils, grow plants on ridges to improve drainage. Avoid frost pockets and windy sites.

HOW TO GROW

Water plants well in summer, to avoid powdery mildew, and harvest fruit regularly. Remove runners, and pot up for new plants (see Propagating strawberries from runners, page 94).

GROWING TIP

Wild strawberries are short-lived but grow easily from seed (see Growing wild strawberries from seed, page 98). They will fruit in their first summer.

WELL TRAVELLED

Archaeological excavations suggest that wild strawberries were eaten in the Stone Age and their seeds were later taken along the Silk Road to Europe, where they were widely grown until the garden strawberry (see page 92) replaced them in popularity in the late eighteenth century.

NOTABLE CULTIVARS

- 'Alexandria' has a long cropping season and a strong, sweet flavour.
- 'Fraise des Bois' bears lots of small, good-flavoured fruit.
- 'Mignonette' produces masses of delicately flavoured fruit.
- 'Rügen' bears lots of large, aromatic berries.
- 'Yellow Wonder' has very sweet fruit that is ignored by birds.

Goji berry

Lycium barbarum aka wolfberry, Duke of Argyll's tea-tree

Family	Solanaceae
Height and spread	3 x 3m/10 x 10ft
Hardiness	Zone 5
Position	Full sun
Harvest	Autumn

These nutritious, red berries can be eaten fresh, dried or cooked and are high in vitamin C and antioxidants. Produced on deciduous, hardy, self-fertile shrubs, they are an increasingly popular fruit crop. The berries follow dainty, purple flowers.

—

WHERE TO GROW

Gojis are easy to grow and tolerant of a wide range of situations from coastal to drought, provided they are in full sun (they will grow in partial shade but crop less). They prefer free-draining soil, so add plenty of bulky organic matter to heavy soil.

HOW TO GROW

Plants are best grown trained against a wall or fence and pruned in spring, as gojis flower and fruit on the previous year's growth. Feed with a general fertilizer at the start of the growing season and with a high-potash liquid feed every two weeks once flowers appear.

GROWING TIP

Handling can turn the berries black so harvest them by gently shaking the fruit on to a sheet laid on the ground beneath the plant.

DIFFERENT PURPOSE
Gojis were introduced to the UK by the Duke of Argyll in 1730, but the plant was initially grown for hedging and ornamental use rather than for its fruit.

NOTABLE CULTIVARS

- 'Big Lifeberry' produces extra-large berries that are delicious when eaten fresh.
- 'Sweet Lifeberry' is reliable, and has berries that are super-sweet when dried.

Growing wild strawberries from seed

Wild strawberries are delightful, little plants that produce small fruit with a fragrant, very distinctive flavour that is quite different to the strawberries that are available in shops. They are perfect for growing in containers and also make pretty edging plants to borders in both the ornamental and the edible garden.

Seeds can be shop-bought or collected from your own plants, as most wild strawberries should come true from seed. Sow indoors in spring or autumn in small pots or seed trays filled with a sieved multipurpose potting compost or a seed compost such as John Innes No. 1. Firm down the compost with your fingertips, and water so that the compost is moist. Thinly scatter the seeds across the surface of the compost, then lightly cover with a sprinkling of sharp sand or sieved compost. Place on a windowsill or in a greenhouse and cover with a pane of glass, or else cover each pot with a clear plastic bag and seal with a rubber band, to increase humidity and help germination.

Wild strawberries need a constant temperature of 18–21°C/65–70°F, so a pot positioned above a radiator may be suitable but germination can still be slow and erratic.

Once seedlings have developed roots and two true leaves, prick them out individually and later pot on into individual small pots. Grow on the young plants, and in late spring plant in the garden having hardened them off first. Do this by leaving the plants outside during the day and bringing them back indoors again at night, for about two weeks, to get them used to temperatures and conditions outside.

1 Scatter wild strawberry seeds thinly across the surface of the compost and grow on in a greenhouse or on a windowsill. Prick out seedlings once they have two true leaves.
2 Once young plants have developed a good root system and are growing strongly, pot on into individual pots.
3 After hardening off autumn- and spring-sown plants for a couple of weeks, plant out in late spring.
4 Wild strawberries are perpetual fruiting, which means they flower and fruit all through the growing season, producing a constant but small crop.
5 Strawberries are ripe once they are an even red all over and have a sweet aroma. Pull them gently from the plant as they bruise easily.

Passion fruit

Passiflora edulis aka granadilla

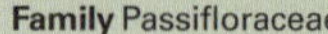

Family Passifloraceae

Height and spread 3 x 2.5m/10 x 8ft

Hardiness Zone 1a

Position Full sun or semi-shade and sheltered

Harvest Late summer–autumn

Vigorous, self-fertile, evergreen climbers such as passion fruits are eye-catching, with their exotic-looking flowers followed by drooping, purple or orange fruit. Passion fruit is native to South America and is common in the tropics and subtropics.

—

WHERE TO GROW

Grow in reasonably fertile, well-drained, moisture-retentive soil. They need a minimum temperature of 5–7°C/41–45°F so are best grown indoors or under glass in cool-temperate areas. Plants do well against a wall. They also grow in pots at least 35cm/14in in diameter.

HOW TO GROW

Although plants climb by self-clinging tendrils they are best grown as a fan and supported by trellis or wires. Prune in spring, just before plants come back into growth, taking side shoots back to two or three shoots.

Give plants a high-potash liquid feed every couple of weeks in spring and summer. Water well, particularly plants grown in pots. Keep conditions humid for the best crop, and pollinate flowers by hand, particularly when temperatures fall below 16°C/61°F. Replace plants after six or seven years.

GROWING TIP

The plump, egg-shaped fruit is ready to harvest once it starts to shrivel. Scoop out the fragrant, runny flesh and crunchy seeds and enjoy on their own or in fruit salads and puddings.

ONE TO AVOID

The winter-hardy, ornamental species *P. caerulea*, which is grown in cool-temperate climates, does produce fruit but it is bland and insipid and not worth eating.

RELIGIOUS TOKEN

The name passion fruit was given by missionaries in Brazil, who used the parts of the flower to illustrate the passion of Christ when converting the indigenous population.

NOTABLE CULTIVARS

- 'Crackerjack' flowers freely and bears large, fragrant, dark purple fruit.
- *f. flavicarpa* has larger, bright yellow fruit that is smooth and glossy and can grow to the size of a grapefruit.
- 'Frederick' bears purple flowers and abundant, purple fruit.
- 'Golden Nugget' is free-flowering, with sweet, canary-yellow fruit .
- 'Panama Red' has white-and-purple flowers followed by large, richly flavoured, red-skinned fruit.
- 'Purple Giant' has very large fruit with deep purple skin and delicious, sweet pulp.

Blackcurrant

Ribes nigrum

Self-fertile and easy-to grow, shrubby blackcurrants are famous for their vitamin-rich, tartly flavoured juice high in vitamin C and phytochemicals. Varieties can be sweet enough to eat from the bush, while others are better cooked and made into pies, jams and jelly.

–

WHERE TO GROW

Although tolerant of a wide range of soils, blackcurrants prefer a fertile, well-drained but moisture-retentive spot. They can cope with light shade, but grow and crop best in full sun. Compact blackcurrants such as 'Ben Sarek' can also be grown in containers of 40cm/16in diameter.

HOW TO GROW

Blackcurrants are best grown as multi-stemmed bushes that are hard pruned every winter – cutting away a third of the older growth down to the base. Plant between autumn and spring and immediately cut all stems down to 2cm/5cm above the soil, to encourage strong young fruiting growth for the following year – bushes fruit on young wood. They are hungry, thirsty plants so mulch with well-rotted manure in spring, and keep them well-watered.

GROWING TIP

Harvest blackcurrants by cutting the bunches, or strigs, of fruit once they ripen. The longer you leave them on the bush the sweeter they get. Older varieties ripen at different times across the plant and, therefore, need to be painstakingly harvested individually as they mature.

JOSTABERRY

This delicious cross between a blackcurrant and a gooseberry tastes more like a gooseberry when young and like a sweetish blackcurrant when ripe. Plants are vigorous and thornless.

USEFUL SUBSTITUTE
During the Second World War, when supplies of fruit high in vitamin C such as oranges were difficult to access, blackcurrants were cultivated and their syrup given free to all children under two. Even now, almost all the commercial crops of blackcurrants in the UK are grown for juice drinks.

NOTABLE CULTIVARS

- 'Ben Connan' is small, early ripening, with large berries; good for small gardens.
- 'Ben Hope' has lots of aromatic, tasty, late-season fruit.
- 'Ben Lomond' is upright, with lots of fruit later in the season.
- 'Ben Sarek' is a mid-season, compact variety, with large, tart berries.
- 'Ben Tirran' is late-cropping, with vigorous, compact growth.
- 'Big Ben' is vigorous, with huge fruit early in the season.

Redcurrant, whitecurrant and pinkcurrant

Ribes rubrum

Close relatives of the blackcurrant, red-, white- and pinkcurrants are self-fertile shrubs dripping with tassels of fruit in summer. They also have nectar-rich flowers and heart-shaped leaves. Whitecurrants are slightly smaller and less sharp than red ones, while pinkcurrants are the sweetest of all and have a delicate fragrance. All are delicious in jams, jellies, puddings and sauces as well as fresh; they freeze well, too.

–

BOTH THE SAME
Whitecurrants are simply albino forms of redcurrants and not a different botanical species, despite often being sold as a separate species.

WHERE TO GROW

All currants are sweeter and riper when grown in full sun but plants tolerate light shade and grow well against walls. They are happy in well-drained, fertile soil, and can also be grown in containers of 40cm/16in diameter.

HOW TO GROW

Grow as open-centred bushes or train into fans, cordons, standards and stepovers (see Restricted tree forms, page 28).

Mulch plants in winter with well-rotted manure and keep well-watered in dry summers. Support plants with twines and canes before they grow heavy with fruit. Net fruit against birds, or use bird scarers, to ensure you can enjoy your harvest when it is fully ripe and deliciously sweet.

Harvest currants only when they are ripe and sweet – they take longer to ripen than you may think, looking ready before they are actually at their best. Cut or nip whole bunches from the plant and then run a fork down them to remove the currants. They

NOTABLE CULTIVARS

Redcurrant

- 'Jonkheer van Tets' is early ripening, with masses of sweet-tasting fruit.
- 'Red Lake' is vigorous, bearing long bunches of large, juicy currants in mid-season.
- 'Redstart' is a heavy-cropping, late-season variety, with an upright shape and bunches of bright fruit.
- 'Rovada' bears late-ripening, translucent fruit on long bunches.
- 'Stanza' is ideal for frost-prone areas, thanks to its late flowering.

Whitecurrant

- 'Blanka' has lots of very large fruit.
- 'Versailles Blanche' is reliable, with high yields of pale yellow fruit in midsummer.
- 'White Grape' produces huge, sweet berries that ripen early in the season.

Pinkcurrant

- 'Gloire de Sablons' bears heavy crops of large, sweetly aromatic, pink fruit.
- 'Rossalin' has deep pink berries on heavy-cropping bushes.

freeze well when spread out on trays; then bag them up.

GROWING TIP

Currants fruit on old wood and at the base of new wood so prune plants in winter, cutting new growth back to two buds to encourage fruiting spurs; also take out any older, dead and diseased wood. Then in early summer cut back all new growth to just two buds, to keep plants compact. Prune trained forms such as fans in early spring, cutting back new wood by a quarter. Alternate cuts each year on opposite sides of the stem, to keep it straight.

Gooseberry

Ribes uva-crispa

Although rarely seen for sale in the shops, gooseberries are easy-to-grow, flavoursome berries that have long featured in cottage gardens thanks to their heavy cropping. There are more than 100 varieties of these self-fertile shrubs, including culinary, dessert and dual-purpose cultivars.

–

Family Grossulariaceae

Height and spread 1–1.5 x 1–1.5m/3–5 x 3–5ft

Hardiness Zone 6

Position Sunny and sheltered

Harvest Late spring (when green) or mid- to late summer (when fully ripe)

WHERE TO GROW

Gooseberries love a sunny, sheltered spot and growing in moist but well-drained, fertile soil. Avoid shallow, poorer soils, which can dry out easily and cause mildew and frost pockets. Early frosts can reduce crops. Plants tolerate shade but harvests will be reduced.

HOW TO GROW

Grow as bushes or standards, train against a wall or grow in a pot. Add plenty of well-rotted manure before planting. Give a balanced feed in winter, and inspect leaves in spring for sawfly larvae and pick any off. Water through dry periods, and net the ripening fruit against the birds. Wrench suckers away at the base by hand rather than cutting them, which encourages regrowth. Gooseberries fruit on old wood and at the base of new wood so need pruning both in winter, cutting back new growth to one or two buds, and in summer, shortening shoots back to five leaves.

GROWING TIP

Harvest twice a year, gathering unripe berries in late spring to early summer. Pick every other one and use for making jam, pies and more. Allow the remaining fruit to swell and ripen on the plant; it will be ready for harvesting later in summer and for eating fresh in tangy desserts.

RIBES DIVARICATUM

Known as Worcesterberry, coast black gooseberry and wild gooseberry, these have tasty, purple, gooseberry-like fruit with excellent resistance to mildew.

CONTINUING COMPETITION
Throughout the UK, gooseberry clubs compete to see who can grow the biggest and heaviest berry. The largest so far from the 'Montrose' variety was the size of a hen's egg.

NOTABLE CULTIVARS

- 'Careless' is an old, heavy-cropping, white variety.
- 'Greenfinch' is a less spiny, new variety, with green berries that are best cooked.
- 'Hinnonmäki Röd' is a new variety with large, sweet, purple-red berries.
- 'Invicta' is a new variety with good disease resistance; its big, green berries are suitable for both culinary and dessert uses.
- 'Leveller' is an old variety that bears heavy crops of golden yellow fruit.

Blackberry and hybrid berries

Rubus fruticosus aka brambles, caneberry

Modern cultivated blackberries produce bumper crops of bigger, juicier berries than their wild cousins, which are gleefully foraged in the countryside. The cultivars are also often thornless and have a more upright habit, making them easier to pick, train and keep in check.

Their hybrids, including tayberries, loganberries and boysenberries, are all deliciously different (see box, below) but well worth growing, particularly as none of them is usually available to buy in shops.

Family Rosaceae

Height and spread 2–3 x 2–3m/7–10 x 7–10ft

Hardiness Zone 6

Position Warm, sunny and sheltered

Harvest Midsummer–early autumn

—

WHERE TO GROW

Blackberries and hybrid berries are happy in any soil and in exposed or shady conditions, although, like most fruit, they crop better if in a sunny, sheltered spot. There are also compact blackberry varieties that thrive in containers.

HOW TO GROW

Immediately after planting, cut canes down to 30cm/12in from the ground. These vigorous, self-fertile plants can then be left to ramble, but you will get more fruit if plants are trained on to wires or into fans. Mulch plants with organic matter in spring, and water plants well in dry summers. After harvesting, cut all fruited canes down to the base and tie the new, replacement canes to the wires.

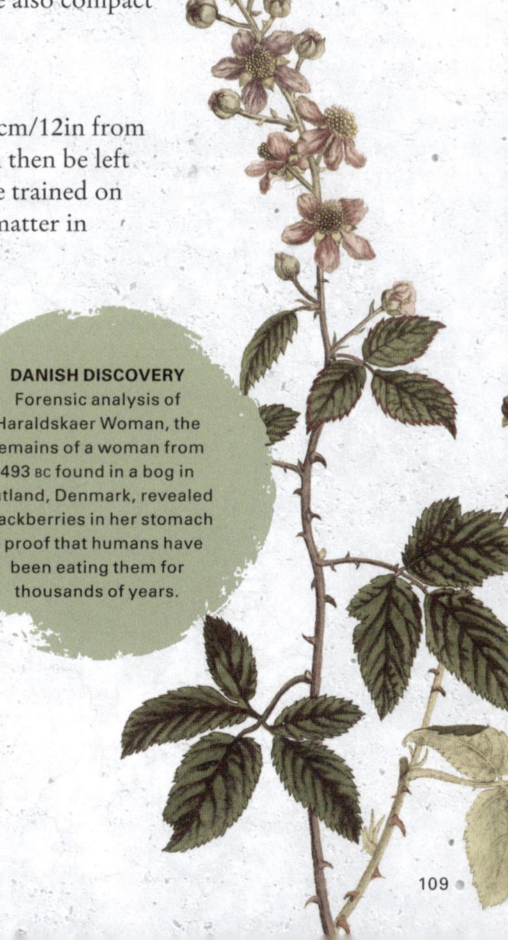

DANISH DISCOVERY

Forensic analysis of Haraldskaer Woman, the remains of a woman from 493 BC found in a bog in Jutland, Denmark, revealed blackberries in her stomach – proof that humans have been eating them for thousands of years.

HYBRID BERRIES

Tayberries (*R.* Tayberry Group) are a cross between a blackberry and a raspberry and named after the River Tay in Scotland. Loganberries (*R.* × *loganobaccus*) are a cross between a blackberry and a raspberry, and have dark red, juicy, sharp-flavoured fruit. Boysenberries (*R.* boysenberry thornless) are a complex hybrid between a loganberry, a raspberry, an American dewberry and a blackberry, with a succulent blackberry flavour.

GROWING TIP

Blackberries ripen gradually across the plant so need harvesting regularly. Unlike raspberries (see page 112), blackberries separate from the plant when ripe, taking the plug with them (raspberries leave it behind).

NOTABLE CULTIVARS

Blackberry

- 'Fantasia' is very vigorous, with lots of deliciously flavoured fruit.
- 'Helen' bears masses of large, early fruit on thornless plants.
- 'Loch Ness' is high yielding, with glossy, tasty fruit.
- 'OregonThornless' is a popular variety, with juicy, flavoursome fruit.

Hybrid berries

- Boysenberry thornless is much less vigorous than other hybrids and is ideal for growing in a large pot.
- 'Buckingham' is a thornless tayberry, with dark red fruit when fully ripe.
- 'Ly 654' is a thornless loganberry; leave fruit to fully ripen before picking.

Raspberry

Rubus idaeus

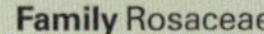

Family Rosaceae

Height and spread 1.8–2 x 1.8–2m/6–7 x 6–7ft

Hardiness Zone 6

Position Sunny and sheltered

Harvest Midsummer–autumn

Easy-to-grow and eternally popular raspberries have a distinctive, sharp-but-sweet taste. They are delicious fresh but also freeze well, and they can be made into jams, puddings and fruit leather (see page 114). For a long, tasty cropping season there are both summer- and autumn-fruiting varieties – summer canes (stems) fruiting in their second year, autumn ones in their first.

–

WHERE TO GROW

Although tolerant of most soils apart from very alkaline, raspberries thrive in a moist, sunny and sheltered spot. Add bulky organic matter to lighter soils, to help retain moisture through summer. These plants also grow happily in containers.

HOW TO GROW

Self-fertile raspberries are usually planted in rows and trained along wires, but a single plant can also be grown up a support. Mulch plants in spring and keep them well-watered once fruit have started to swell, watering at the base to avoid fungal diseases. Remove suckers at the base.

GROWING TIP

Summer-fruiting canes crop on the previous season's wood so cut fruited canes down to the ground after fruiting and tie the remaining healthy canes to their support. Autumn-fruiting canes, which fruit on the current season's growth, should be cut down to the ground in late winter.

NOTABLE CULTIVARS

Summer fruiting

- 'Glen Ample' is a mid-season, thornless variety, with large, delicious fruit.
- 'Glen Magna' has late-season, large fruit.
- 'Glen Moy' is an early, thornless, heavily cropping variety.
- Ruby Beauty ('NR7') is an early season, compact raspberry; ideal for a container.
- 'Tulameen' is mid- to late-season fruiting, with large, sweet berries.

Autumn fruiting

- 'All Gold' bears tasty, yellow fruit, which birds helpfully seem to avoid.
- 'Autumn Bliss' has medium-sized, deep red fruit.
- 'Joan J' develops an upright, productive plant, with full-flavoured fruit.
- 'Polka' bears large, flavoursome berries until the first frosts.

MULTI-FRUITS

Raspberries are actually a cluster of drupelets rather than a fruit – each individual bump is a fruit with its own seed inside and connected to the next bump by fine hairs.

Raspberry fruit leather

Raspberries are delicious fruit that have a limited and expensive season in the shops and, apart from freezing, do not store or last long. They do, however, make a sweet and tasty fruit leather – those little rolls of dried fruit that last for weeks in an airtight container and are a great way of giving yourself and the kids a vitamin boost long after the harvest is over.

Lots of other fruits – apples, apricots, peaches, nectarines, plums, strawberries and other berries – work really well too, both on their own or in combination. Whichever fruit you use, you just need to make a thick, smooth purée, which is dried slowly into a soft leather. Although this may take a relatively long time, the process is really easy and most of the work is actually done overnight.

Preheat the oven to a very low setting such as 75°C or 170°F. Put washed raspberries in a saucepan with an equal amount of chopped and peeled apples and cook gently until pulpy. Add honey to taste, if you wish. Allow the purée to cool a little before pushing it through a sieve. Then spread the mixture evenly and thinly over a baking sheet lined with lightly oiled greaseproof paper, tipping it at either end to help the mix spread across the whole sheet. Place in the oven and leave to dry for about ten hours or overnight. The leather should be a little tacky, but not sticky, and peel off the greaseproof paper easily. Once cooled, cut into strips or other shapes, peel off the greaseproof paper and then roll them up. Raspberry fruit leather will keep in a sealed container for around three months and can be frozen for up to six months.

1 Pick your raspberries or other fruit when they are totally ripe. You will need about 500g/1lb 2oz for a baking sheet's worth of raspberry fruit leather.
2 Put the washed raspberries and apples in a pan and cook over a low heat until they have broken down into a pulp.
3 Raspberries and berries such as blackberries contain a lot of seeds and need sieving once they have softened into a pulp.
4 Spread the mixture thinly over the lined baking sheet. Once dry, the mixture will be bright, bendy and leathery.
5 Allow the fruit leather to cool, then cut into strips or other shapes and roll up.

1

2

3

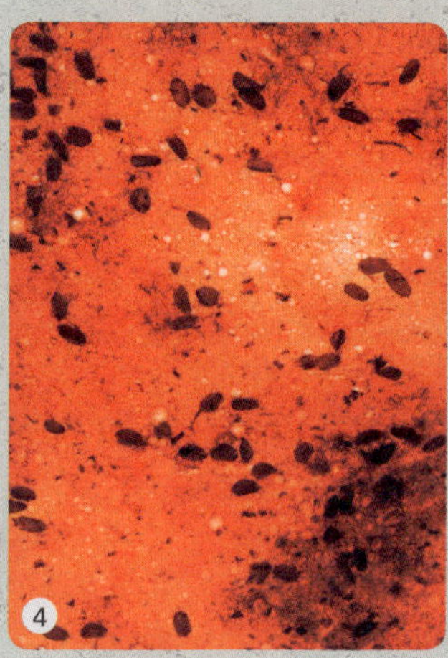
4

5

Blueberry

Vaccinium spp.

Blueberries are beautiful plants producing tasty, highly nutritious berries that follow bell-shaped blossoms; many also have breathtaking autumn leaf colour. The main blueberries grown are the northern highbush (*V. corymbosum*) and the lowbush blueberry (*V. angustifolium*). Both offer a range of fruiting seasons, making it possible to eat fresh blueberries from midsummer through to autumn. Some varieties are self-fertile but all crop better if grown with more than one plant.

–

WHERE TO GROW

Easy-to-grow blueberries need moist, acid soil and grow very happily in ericaceous compost in a pot if your garden has alkaline soil (see Blueberries in a pot, page 118).

HOW TO GROW

Keep plants well-watered with rainwater (never tap water), and mulch with acidic materials such as bark chippings or pine needles. Net berries as soon as they appear, to protect them from birds. Blueberries ripen gradually across the plant, so harvest every few days when each berry is a deep purple colour. Prune plants in winter, to encourage strong, new growth, and feed with a lime-free fertilizer in spring.

GROWING TIP

Blueberries need acid soil so check the pH of the soil each spring. Add sulphur chippings, if necessary, to lower the pH to 5.5 or below.

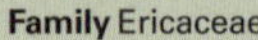

Family Ericaceae

Height and spread 1.5–2 x 1.5m/5–7 x 5ft

Hardiness Zone 6

Position Sunny and sheltered

Harvest Midsummer–autumn

NOTABLE CULTIVARS

Highbush

- 'Bluecrop' (self-fertile) is a reliable cropper, with large, tasty fruit in midsummer.
- 'Duke' (self-fertile) is a bushy plant that flowers late and crops early, making it good for cool-temperate regions.
- 'Nelson' (self-fertile) bears large, tasty fruit.
- 'Pink Lemonade' (self-fertile) produces mild-flavoured, deep pink fruit.
- 'Spartan' is an early to mid-season variety, with tangy berries; needs another blueberry nearby to crop well.
- 'Sunshine Blue' (self-fertile) is a dense, stocky plant; ideal for container growing.

Lowbush

- 'Chippewa' (self-fertile) is a hardy, compact plant with large, sky-blue berries.

BOOST TO THE SYSTEM
Often touted as a superfood, blueberries are, just like other berries, a great source of vitamin C and rich in phytochemicals such as anthocyanidins and antioxidants, which are reported to be effective against a number of health conditions.

Blueberries in a pot

One of the joys of growing fruit in pots is that you can grow whatever you wish, regardless of the soil you have in your garden – in a container you can tailor the compost to give crops exactly what they need.

Blueberries can be tricky plants as they need a light, moist and, most importantly, acidic soil but this makes them the perfect crop for container growing. They are also beautiful plants with dinky bell-shaped flowers, good autumn leaf colour and delicious fruit that range in colour from dusty purple to pink to green all at the same time.

If you only have room for one blueberry, be sure to grow a self-fertile variety such as 'Nelson' or 'Sunshine Blue' that is able to crop on its own, but if you have the space it is well worth growing another plant to guarantee a successful and productive crop.

Always use an ericaceous compost as ordinary potting compost is too alkaline and will eventually kill the plant. After planting, use an acidic mulch such as bark or pine needles spread on top of the compost to help it retain moisture.

Water the plant well and keep the compost moist, using rainwater if possible. Tap water tends to be alkaline and will gradually neutralize the compost and weaken the plant. Place your blueberry in a warm, sunny spot, keeping an eye on watering in hot weather. Protect the berries from greedy birds and remember that blueberries ripen at different times so keep checking and picking so you do not miss any fruit.

1. Blueberries prefer a free-draining soil so mix one part grit with two parts ericaceous potting compost.
2. Water the plant well before positioning in the centre of the pot at the same level it was in its previous container.
3. Keep the compost moist, particularly in warm weather and use rainwater if you can rather than tap water, which tends to be alkaline.
4. As soon as the flowers start to fade, protect plants from the birds with netting, held away from the fruit so that the birds cannot peck through it.

Cranberry

Vaccinium macrocarpon aka American cranberry, large cranberry, bearberry

These low-growing, self-fertile evergreens are smothered in little, pink flowers followed by juicy, dark red berries and are at home in the boggy moorlands of northern USA. If you replicate these conditions at home, plants should start to fruit from their third year.

–

Family Ericaceae

Height and spread 20 x 200cm/8–84in

Hardiness Zone 6

Position Sun or partial shade

Harvest Autumn

WHERE TO GROW

Plants need wet but not waterlogged, acidic soil; such conditions are easier to control by growing plants in ericaceous compost in a pot. Alternatively, dig a special bed and line it with perforated plastic.

HOW TO GROW

Saturate the compost before planting and then mulch plants with sand. Prune lightly after harvesting, to encourage vigorous, upright growth that will produce more fruit.

GROWING TIP

Keep plants constantly moist by collecting and watering plants regularly with rainwater, which has a lower pH than tap water.

WATERY HARVEST

Commercially grown cranberries are kept moist in the growing season and then flooded to ease harvest – the berries float and are then skimmed from the surface.

NOTABLE CULTIVARS

- 'Early Black' is early fruiting, and produces large, juicy, purple-red berries.
- 'Pilgrim' has evergreen foliage that turns bronze in winter; good for containers.
- 'Red Star' is a vigorous plant with large fruits.
- 'Stevens' has firm, juicy and sweeter berries than other varieties.

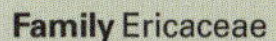

Lingonberry

Vaccinium vitis-idaea aka cowberry, mountain cranberry, whortleberry

Lingonberries are low-growing, evergreen plants with juicy, tart, red fruit similar to cranberries (see page 120), but they are much easier to grow and often fruit twice in a year. Although self-fertile, they will produce a bigger crop if there is more than one plant. Lingonberries have attractive, pink flowers and are perfect for container growing.

Family Ericaceae

Height and spread 20 x 20cm/8 x 8in

Hardiness Zone 6

Position Sun or partial shade

Harvest Midsummer–early autumn

WHERE TO GROW

Lingonberries prefer gritty, free-draining, acid soil or ericaceous compost. They crop better in a sunny site.

HOW TO GROW

Keep plants moist by watering with rainwater, which has a lower pH than tap water. Prune out old wood in autumn or winter, to encourage new fruiting wood. Lingonberries take a couple of years to fruit.

GROWING TIP

Mulch with bark to prevent the soil pH from rising and to keep weeds down.

FROM THE WILD

Native to Scandinavia, lingonberries are a popular foraged fruit and a key ingredient in jams, sauces and many traditional dishes.

NOTABLE CULTIVARS

- 'Ida' is a dwarf variety that is ideal for container growing.
- Koralle Group is a neat, bushy plant with large, juicy fruit.
- 'Red Pearl' is vigorous and high yielding.

Grape

Vitis vinifera aka grapevine, cultivated grapes

Fortunately, these stunning, self-fertile, climbing vines, with their large leaves, can be grown in even the smallest space. Encourage them to climb over a wall or fence or train them as a standard in a pot. There are grapes for eating freshly picked (known as dessert grapes) and grapes for making wine.

–

Family Vitaceae

Height and spread 12 x 2.5–4m/40 x 8–13ft

Hardiness Zone 5

Position Full sun and sheltered

Harvest Late summer–mid-autumn

WHERE TO GROW

Wine grapes can be grown outside in a warm, sunny sheltered spot such as against a wall or fence. Dessert grapes need warmth and sun and should be grown in a greenhouse in cool-temperate climates or they can be planted outside and then trained under glass. They like free-draining soil, but otherwise are tolerant of most soil types.

CHAIN REACTION
Yeasts occur naturally on grape skin and begin fermenting as soon as the grapes are crushed, converting the sugars to alcohol.

HOW TO GROW

Grapes are vigorous climbers and need training either on the guyot system (with one or two fruiting stems trained along a main wire in opposite directions) or as a cordon (one or multiple stems with fruiting side shoots trained on to wires spaced at intervals across a wall or fence). If space is limited or if grown in a pot, grapes can also be trained as a standard on a tall, clear stem.

Water plants well in dry periods in their first year. Remove all flowers in the first two years; allow only three bunches on three-year-old plants. Thereafter, leave plants to flower and fruit freely.

Once tiny grapes appear, start to feed with a high-potash liquid fertilizer; also protect them from birds and wasps with netting. Thin bunches when grapes are pea-sized, by removing one in three grapes, so that the rest can swell further. To ensure grapes ripen fully, nip out any leaves around

the fruit so that the sunlight can reach the grapes.

Grapes are ready when they are soft. However, their taste will give you a better idea – they should be sweet and sugary.

Grape vines produce fruit on one-year-old wood so need pruning each year. They bleed sap profusely when in growth, so prune when dormant in late winter. Reduce side shoots on cordons and standards back to two buds, and on guyots to three or four buds.

GROWING TIP

Mulching around the base of the vine with white pebbles or gravel not only helps to suppress weeds and holds in moisture, but also reflects sunlight into the canopy. Alternatively, a darker mulch will absorb the heat of the sun and warm up the soil. Do not use an organic mulch such as manure, because this increases fertility and leads to more green growth and less fruit.

NOTABLE CULTIVARS

Dessert

- 'Boskoop Glory' is an outdoor variety, with fine-flavoured, black grapes.
- 'Buckland Sweetwater' is compact, with sweet, early-cropping, white fruit.
- 'Muscat of Alexandria' has white grapes, which need warmth to ripen well.
- 'Shiava Grossa', aka Black Hamburgh, is vigorous and grows outside as well as under cover; produces sweet, dark red fruit.

Wine

- 'Bacchus' is a white grape with a distinctive flavour; can be grown outdoors in cool-temperate regions.
- 'Pinot Noir' needs a cool-temperate climate for its red grapes to ripen fully.
- 'Seyval Blanc' is a reliable, white grape variety, with good disease resistance.

Nuts

Pecan

Carya illinoinensis

Large and elegantly beautiful pecans are slow-growing trees requiring patience and space but little else. They are brilliantly easy and undemanding. Although self-fertile, they are best grown with another pecan tree nearby.

–

Family Juglandaceae

Height and spread 30 x 20m/100 x 66ft

Hardiness Zone 6

Position Full sun and sheltered

Harvest Autumn

WHERE TO GROW

These immense trees are suitable for only the largest gardens, where they prefer rich, well-drained soil and shelter from strong winds.

HOW TO GROW

Grow as a standard with a central leader. During their first three or four years trees appear to grow very little while they concentrate on putting down a long taproot, so keep the base of the tree weed-free and do not let the soil dry out. Feed with a balanced fertilizer each spring. Cut out any congested or crossing wood in winter.

GROWING TIP

Choose grafted cultivars that will harvest within the fourth year from planting. Pecans are ready to harvest once the husk starts to split. They can be kept in a refrigerator or a freezer, where they will last six months.

NOTABLE CULTIVARS

- 'Carlson No. 3' is a 'northern' variety for cool-temperate regions; it flowers and fruits early, producing small, oblong, tasty nuts.
- 'Desirable' is reliable, with lots of large, rounded, tasty pecans.
- 'Lucas' is a hardy, heavy-yielding tree for northern regions, producing rich, deliciously flavoured, small pecans.
- 'Mohawk' produces huge pecans in 5–7 years; is suitable for warm areas.
- 'Mullahy' is another 'northern' variety for cool-temperate regions, with large, tasty nuts.

USEFUL CHANGES

Native to the southern states of North America, new, hardier pecan varieties have been bred with greater frost resistance and less need for a long, warm summer.

Sweet chestnut

Castanea sativa aka European chestnut, Spanish chestnut

Autumn-ripening sweet chestnuts are easy-to-grow, long-lived, productive trees suitable only for large gardens. Few trees are self-fertile so grow at least two varieties. Sweet chestnuts can be slow to fruit – look for new, grafted varieties that crop within three or four years. The nutritionally rich nuts store well and for a long time, once dried.

Family Fagaceae

Height and spread 12 x 8m/40 x 26ft

Hardiness Zone 6

Position Full sun

Harvest Autumn

–

WHERE TO GROW

Plant in well-drained, fertile soil; avoid waterlogged or chalky soil. Trees will not fruit when grown in shade.

HOW TO GROW

Water trees well in dry weather in summer, when nuts are forming. Prune trees only in their first few years, to create an open shape; do this in winter.

GROWING TIP

Gather nuts regularly when they fall – before squirrels and other animals get your crop. Wear gloves to remove them from their spiky burrs, then leave the chestnuts to dry for a few days, for a sweeter flavour.

SPECIAL OCCASIONS

Once a staple food in Europe, sweet chestnuts are often enjoyed just as a delicacy today – especially at Christmas when they are used in stuffings (see Chestnut stuffing, page 128) and puddings.

NOTABLE CULTIVARS

- 'Marigoule' produces large, dark red nuts within a couple of years of planting.
- 'Marron de Lyon' is reliable; produces large nuts within three years.
- 'Regal' reaches just 5m/16ft in ten years; bears delicious nuts in two or three years.

Chestnut stuffing

A classic festive ingredient, shiny chestnuts are rustic and versatile, delicious in both sweet and savoury recipes. Equally tasty in soups, stews and roast dinners as they are in puddings and cakes, they taste even better when they are home-grown! Stuffing, an integral part of every festive meal, is a delicious way to enjoy your home-grown bounty; just mix them with herbs, breadcrumbs and sausage meat and then roast.

Ensure the quality of the nuts by watering your tree if the weather is dry in the few weeks leading up to harvest. Once ripe the nuts will start to fall from the tree and the harvest should last a couple of weeks, so you will need to check your tree every few days. Harvest your crop quickly or the squirrels will get them! Unfortunately, both the nuts and the leaves fall at the same time and it can be a painstaking and back-breaking job finding them among the leaf fall.

Chestnuts have a very high water content as they are picked when they are still living seeds, which means they will deteriorate very quickly. Dry them for a couple of days outside in the sun if you can or indoors; they can then be kept in the fridge for a few weeks. Chestnuts are never eaten raw but must be cooked first either by boiling or roasting. Slit the shell of each chestnut carefully with a sharp knife first or it will explode when it cooks. Once they are cooked remove the shell and papery skin and they are ready to add to your favourite stuffing recipe.

1. Chestnuts ripen in autumn and are ready for harvesting once the spiky husk starts to split open.
2. Roast chestnuts by scattering them into a large pan and heating them on an open fire or in the oven until the skins split open.
3. Peel chestnuts when they are still warm to ensure the entire shells and furry skins, which are very bitter, are removed.
4. Earthy chestnuts chopped into stuffing are an integral ingredient for many a festive meal.

Cobnut

Corylus avellana

Cobnuts are a cultivated hazelnut characterized by the distinctive, papery husks that clothe the nuts. Native to Europe and Western Asia, they are grown for their nuts and coppiced wood. Although self-fertile, they will produce a bigger crop if more than one tree is planted.

–

Family Betulaceae

Height and spread 6 x 5m/20 x 16ft

Hardiness Zone 6

Position Full sun and sheltered

Harvest Late summer

WHERE TO GROW

These trees tolerate a wide range of soils provided they have a pH of 5–7.5 and are well-drained. They need a sheltered spot in full sun as both the male and female flowers appear in late winter or very early spring.

HOW TO GROW

Cobnuts are best grown as multi-stemmed trees, in groups to maximize pollination. Topdress with a general fertilizer in spring. Prune regularly to promote nut-bearing wood, removing older, thicker stems in late winter.

GROWING TIP

To encourage flower buds, brut (snap in half but without completely breaking off) a few new shoots in late summer and leave them hanging on the tree. Shorten these to 10cm/4in in winter.

FEAST FOR WILDLIFE

Ecologically, cobnuts are an important food source for the insects of the order Lepidoptera, which feed on their leaves, as well as for the invertebrates, small mammals (such as squirrels) and birds that eat their nuts.

NOTABLE CULTIVARS

- 'Butler' is vigorous, with delicious, large nuts.
- 'Cosford Cob' bears sweetly flavoured nuts.
- 'Tonda di Giffoni' is compact and high-yielding and produces large nuts.
- 'Pearson's Prolific' is a small tree, with good-flavoured nuts.

Filbert

Corylus maxima

A species of hazel similar to cobnuts is the filbert, but it has a long, papery husk that often covers the nut completely. Filberts are valued for their autumn colour, timber and nuts. These self-fertile, deciduous shrubs produce a bigger crop if more than one filbert is growing in the area.

—

Family Betulaceae

Height and spread 6 x 5m/20 x 16ft

Hardiness Zone 6

Position Sun or partial shade and sheltered

Harvest Late summer

WHERE TO GROW

Filberts crop heaviest in sun. Avoid frost pockets as flowers and catkins are produced early in the year. Filberts grow on all but waterlogged soil.

HOW TO GROW

Mulch in spring with bulky organic matter, and water well in dry seasons. Brut (see Growing tip, page 130) new shoots in summer, to encourage flower buds, and then shorten to 10cm/4in in winter. Prune regularly to encourage nut-bearing wood, by removing the older, thicker stems in late winter.

GROWING TIP

Filberts are best grown as multi-stemmed trees, so when buying choose plants that have already been pruned into multi-stems at the base.

HARVESTING TIP

The name filbert is believed by many to derive from the French feast day of St Philbert's on 20 August, when the nuts are ripe.

NOTABLE CULTIVARS

- 'Gunslebert' is a good, reliable cropper, with tightly hulled nuts that prevent earwig infestation.
- 'Kentish Cob', aka 'Lambert's Filbert', is an old, upright variety.
- 'Purpurea' has claret and crimson foliage, red catkins and lots of nuts.

Walnut

Juglans regia aka English walnut, Persian walnut, common walnut

Such tall, imposing, self-fertile trees are for a large garden. They are easy to grow, and produce large crops of delicious nuts that can be eaten green, 'wet' (fresh) or dried. They produce a even bigger crop if more than one walnut tree is planted in the vicinity.

–

Family Juglandaceae

Height and spread 30 x 15m/100 x 50ft

Hardiness Zone 6

Position Full sun

Harvest Midsummer (green) or early autumn (when fully ripe)

WHERE TO GROW

Walnuts grow best in fertile, well-drained, alkaline soil. Avoid windy sites and frost pockets, as spring frost can damage flowers and foliage.

HOW TO GROW

Plant in autumn or winter and apply a well-balanced fertilizer in spring. Prune when necessary but only from midsummer to autumn to prevent 'bleeding'. Harvest green walnuts in midsummer; otherwise wait until the husks split open, in early autumn, to pick.

GROWING TIP

Always choose the right variety for your region – late-leafing, late-flowering varieties are essential for cool-temperate areas. Opt for grafted varieties, which crop earlier in the tree's life cycle and are more resistant to frost.

PLANTS BEWARE

Walnuts produce the growth-inhibitor juglone, which has a detrimental effect on sensitive plants such as tomatoes and apples grown nearby. English walnut (*J. regia*) is less of a problem than black walnut (*J. nigra*).

NOTABLE CULTIVARS

- 'Broadview' is compact, very hardy, late-leafing and reaches 9m/30ft tall if unpruned.
- 'Buccaneer' is an upright tree that crops from year four, with nuts good for pickling.
- 'Franquette' is a late-leafing, French variety.
- 'Rita' is compact; can be pruned to grow less than 8m/26ft tall.

Almond

Prunus dulcis aka sweet almond, almond oil plant

Almonds are attractive trees with fragrant, pink blossom followed by bunches of green, peach-like fruit, each one containing a delicious nut. Self-fertile and compact almonds are a great addition to the garden, but trees crop more heavily if more than one is grown nearby.

–

Family Rosaceae

Height and spread 4–8 x 4–8m/13–26 x 13–26ft

Hardiness Zone 6

Position Sunny and sheltered

Harvest Late summer

WHERE TO GROW

Harvests will be most bountiful when trees are positioned against a warm, sunny wall. Plant in well-drained, fertile soil.

HOW TO GROW

Choose Marianna 26–24 rootstock and train as an open, freestanding tree or as a fan against a warm wall. Mulch with bulky organic matter in spring, and hand-pollinate blossom if the weather is poor during flowering. Prune in spring or summer, to avoid silver leaf infection.

GROWING TIP

Harvest once the outer husks crack open. Remove the husks and dry the nuts in the sun for a few days. Once dried, the nuts store well.

NOTABLE CULTIVARS

- 'Ingrid' is a reliable almond/peach hybrid, with pink flowers and heavy crops.
- 'Mandaline' (self-fertile) bears high-quality nuts.
- 'Princesse' has early, white flowers and large bunches of nuts; it offers some peach leaf curl resistance.
- 'Robijn' (self-fertile) is a modern almond/peach hybrid, with sweetly flavoured nuts.

FERTILITY BOOST

The world's largest producer of almonds, in California, USA, ensures pollination by renting more than half of the total US honeybee population and trucking them in from across the country to their almond groves.

Troubleshooting

Some problems with pests and diseases are inevitable no matter what you grow, but the best way to deal with them is through prevention. Good growing techniques will help you have strong, healthy fruit trees and other plants that are far less vulnerable to attack. Therefore, always grow fruit in its ideal conditions and give it the best possible start in life.

Keep on top of tasks such as pruning, watering and feeding, and do not overcrowd plants. Encourage beneficial insects and animals such as bees, butterflies and birds into your garden to help you, and, finally, find out which pests and diseases might cause you problems and arm yourself against them. Many chemicals traditionally used in the fight against pest and diseases are no longer legally allowed for use on edible crops. Your local garden centre will know what is still available and is also a good source for biological controls, which work by introducing the natural predators of certain pests.

CULTURAL PROBLEMS

Growing fruit in a less-than-perfect spot or caring for it sporadically can lead to stress and affect the health and productivity of your plants. This may cause the following cultural problems.

Fruit splitting

Inconsistent watering and leaving fruit on the tree too long when it is ripe can cause fruit to split. Cherries, grapes, currants and melons are all susceptible. Water regularly and pick fruit as soon as it is ripe, to avoid it.

Nutrient deficiency

Yellowing of leaves or interveinal yellowing can be signs of inadequate nutrients in the soil or compost or, in the case of acid-loving fruit, that the soil is too alkaline. Feed plants regularly and add sulphur chips to the soil to reduce its pH.

Poor fruit set

This is caused by poor flowering, inadequate pollination and blossom frost damage, so protect flowers against the frost, ensure insects are pollinating and prune regularly and at the right time, as a lack of flowers can be caused by a lack of, or badly timed, pruning.

PESTS AND DISEASES

Be vigilant in spotting problems early and thereby keeping damage to a minimum. Varieties resistant to some fungal diseases are also available.

Aphids

As they attack many fruit in early summer, aphids are most noticeable on young shoot tips. Although the damage they cause is minimal, they can spread viruses. Squash them with your fingers, and encourage ladybirds and other natural predators into the garden.

Birds

Birds love fruit as much as you and I do, but unfortunately this means they have the potential to wipe out an entire crop before you even get a look in. Cherries, currants and berries are all vulnerable so protect plants with tautly placed netting as the flowers fade.

Codling moth
Larvae tunnel into the centre of fruit such as apples and pears to feed, spoiling it as they go and also leaving a wound for other pests such as wasps to attack. Hang pheromone traps in susceptible trees in late spring to catch the males, which then leaves the females unmated.

Gooseberry sawfly
If gooseberries and red- and whitecurrants appear stripped of their leaves in early summer, small, green, sawfly larvae may be the culprits. Attacks can weaken plants, so check plants regularly from late spring for the larvae and pick them off by hand. A biological control is also available, as is a chemical spray.

Mealybug
A problem for citrus and grapes grown under glass is a mealybug infestation. Mealybugs are insects, covered in a fluffy, white wax, that suck the sap from plant leaves. They also excrete a sticky substance that coats foliage and attracts sooty mould. They hide in nooks in plants,making them tricky to get rid of. Infestations can stunt growth and cause poor fruit yields. Inspect plants and introduce the biocontrol *Cryptolaemus* beetles or spray plants with insecticidal soap.

Red spider mite
Look out for red spider mites in a greenhouse on melons, grapes and citrus, but also occasionally on apples

White, fluffy mealybugs are a common problem on grapes, citrus and figs.

and plums. They are sap-sucking mites that attack plant leaves and, in severe cases, can kill plants. Symptoms include yellow mottling of the leaves, leaf fall and fine webbing strung between leaves and plants. Red spider mites love warm, dry conditions so they are a problem only in summer. Keep humidity levels up in a greenhouse by damping down the ground every day in hot weather. Remove infected plants at once, and ensure the greenhouse is cleared and cleaned thoroughly at the end of the season, to stop re-infection next season.

Slugs and snails
A potential problem for strawberries and melons grown outside are slugs and snails. Their familiar slime trails and holes in leaves are telltale signs. Prevent an attack by trapping slugs and snails in beer traps or upturned citrus skins or by sprinkling slug pellets (those containing ferric sulphate rather than metaldehyde are less toxic and harmful to children, animals and wildlife) around the bases of plants. Night-time collecting missions with a torch work well, too.

Avoid wasps damaging your crops by harvesting fruit as soon as it is ripe.

Botrytis can be a problem on soft-fruit crops such as grapes, particularly if humidity is high.

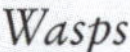

Wasps

From midsummer onwards wasps can be a constant nuisance. They love strawberries, other berry types and grapes, but are also drawn to apples, pears and plums, so harvest fruit as soon as it is ripe. Hang wasp traps of jam diluted with water in trees, and pick up windfalls from the ground.

Winter moth

The caterpillar attacks newly emerging leaves, buds and flowers of fruit trees during spring, particularly those of plums, pears and cherries. Squash eggs by hand between late autumn and spring, or smear a greaseband of petroleum jelly around each trunk in autumn, so that the flightless females cannot walk over it to lay eggs.

DISEASES

Bacterial canker

Affecting the stone fruit cherries, peaches, almonds, nectarines, apricots and plums, as well as apples, canker is a serious problem that can eventually kill trees. Signs of infection include brown spots on leaves, dieback and clear, brown gum oozing from the trunk or branches. Prune back infected branches in summer, as soon as you spot any symptoms. A copper-based fungicide applied in autumn can also work.

Blossom wilt

Stone fruit (cherries, apricots, peaches, nectarines, plums, gages and damsons) and apples and pears are prone to blossom wilt – flowers wither and rot as soon as they emerge but still remain on the tree. Blossom wilt can also spread to the leaves, thereby weakening the tree and making it vulnerable to other problems. Prune back infected stems to healthy tissue or pre-empt an attack by spraying plants with a copper-based fungicide before flowering.

Botrytis

Grey mould (*Botrytis* species) is mostly a problem on soft fruit and grapes, and it causes a grey, fuzzy coating on the fruit and other soft tissue, which eventually die. It is prevalent in high humidity so water plants from below

Coral spot will continue to spread along a stem and become extensive if left unchecked.

Look out for the fuzzy, grey signs of downy mildew, and nip out any infected growth.

and ensure good ventilation in a greenhouse. Cut away infected parts.

Brown rot
Any fruit that has been damaged can suffer from brown rot, which enters the wound and turns the fruit brown and then covers it in round, grey spots. Remove infected fruit, to prevent re-infection.

Coral spot
This disease affects all woody fruit, particularly currants, figs and grapes. Look for raised, orange-pink spots on dead wood, and cut it out straight away as coral spot spreads quickly.

Downy mildew
This plant disease causes blotches and a grey fuzz on the leaves, flowers and fruit of grapes and melons. It thrives in wet weather, so do not overwater plants and always water them at their bases and not over the leaves. Also, do not overcrowd plants so there is good air movement around them. Nip off any infected areas as soon as you spot them.

Fireblight
Members of the Rosaceae family, which includes apples, pears and quince, are vulnerable to fireblight. This bacterial disease causes blackening of leaves, stems and branches. There is no cure, so cut infected growth back to healthy tissue, and sterilize tools when finished.

Rust
Fungi that attack cane fruit and sometimes pear and plum trees, rust can be spotted by the bright orange pustules that appear on leaves in summer. It weakens plants so nip out infected leaves as soon as you spot it.

Silver leaf
Infecting all stone fruit (cherries, apricots, peaches, nectarines, plums, gages and damsons), silver leaf appears as a silver sheen on leaves, which then wither and die. Purple bracket fungi also appear on branches. The fungus enters through pruning cuts, so prune in summer, when the sap is rising and fungal spores are less prevalent, to reduce the risk of infection.

Have fleece at hand in spring ready to protect stone-fruit blossom from early frosts.

Carefully secure the new growth of raspberries with twine tied in a figure of eight.

Harvest cherries as soon as they are ripe and then prune the tree.

As soon as the flowers start to fade, protect strawberries from scavenging birds, with netting.

What to do when

To keep your fruit trees and plants in the very best health and producing heavy crops of tasty fruit, you need to undertake certain jobs at the right time of year. Each season has its own needs, from watering, weeding and feeding to pruning, harvesting and storing. Use these simple calendars to help you to keep on top of the key seasonal tasks.

SPRING

- Mulch around the bases of trees and bushes with a 5cm/2in layer of organic matter, keeping it away from the stems and trunks.
- Repot or topdress fruit grown in containers and give each a general liquid feed.
- Hoe out weeds around fruit plants.
- The beginning of the season is the last chance to plant bare-root plants.

Fruit trees

- Check for forecasts of frost throughout the season, and protect the blossom of stone fruit (cherries, apricots, peaches, nectarines, plums, gages and damsons) with fleece. Remember to remove the protection during the day, so that pollinating insects can access the flowers.
- Remove suckers around the bases of trees by pulling rather than cutting, which can promote regrowth.
- Prune figs.
- Hang up codling moth pheromone traps.
- Harvest loquats.
- Prune almond trees.

Soft fruit

- Sow wild strawberry seed, pot on the seedlings and then plant them out later in the season.
- Protect all strawberries grown in the ground from slugs and snails, and put straw or mats around the bases of plants to protect the fruit when it develops.
- Sow melon seed, potting on later in the season.
- Harvest early-season strawberries and those grown under glass.
- Water fruit in pots, using rainwater for blueberries, cranberries and lingonberries, and check and water newly planted fruit and any grown against a wall.
- Start to tie in and train kiwi fruit stems.
- Train and tie in fan-grown fruit.
- Ensure doors and vents are open on a greenhouse on warm days so that pollinating insects can access plants.
- Brush hands over the flowers of grapes growing under glass, to help pollination.
- Protect all fruit from the birds by covering them with netting once flowers start to fade.
- Harvest gooseberries.
- Keep an eye on red-, pink- and whitecurrants and gooseberries for signs of gooseberry sawfly.

SUMMER

- Hoe out weeds around fruit plants regularly.

- Check plants for drought stress, particularly those that are newly planted, grown in pots or against a wall.
- Begin to feed fruit in pots regularly with a high-potash liquid feed.

Fruit trees

- Move citrus growing under glass outside for summer.
- Thin out citrus fruit.
- Thin apples and pears after the 'June drop' (see Apple, page 57).
- Summer-prune all plants grown as restricted tree forms (see page 28), as well as apples and pears.
- Hang wasp traps in peach, nectarine, apricot, apple, pear, plum, gage and damson trees.
- Harvest cherries, apricots, peaches and nectarines and then prune the trees.
- Harvest plums, gages and damsons and then prune the trees.
- Harvest citrus, pomegranates, mulberries, cobnuts and filberts.
- Harvest early fruiting apples and pears towards the end of the season.
- Brut the new shoots on cobnuts and filberts (see Growing tip, page 130).
- Harvest walnuts and then prune the trees from midsummer.
- Harvest almonds, then prune trees.
- Harvest figs and remove immature fruit.

Soft fruit

- Summer-prune red-, pink- and whitecurrants and gooseberries.
- Summer-prune kiwi fruit, and thin out clusters of grapes. Harvest them when ripe.
- Water and feed melons and thin out the swelling fruit. As the remaining fruit grows, support each one with netting or old tights.
- Harvest strawberries, currants, gooseberries, passion fruit, blackberries and hybrid berries, lingonberries, grapes, melons and blueberries.
- Harvest summer-fruiting raspberries; cut down the canes after cropping and tie in new ones.
- Peg down and grow on strawberry runners for new plants if needed; otherwise, remove all runners.
- Keep an eye out for red spider mite in the greenhouse.

AUTUMN

- Order new bare-root bushes and trees.
- Prepare the ground well and then begin planting new trees and other plants.
- Hoe out weeds around fruit plants regularly.
- Check plants for drought stress, particularly those grown in containers, those planted against a wall and those newly planted.

Fruit trees

- This is the last chance to prune stone-fruit trees.
- Harvest medlars and lay out to blet (see Medlar, page 64).
- Harvest apples and pears and store those in good condition.
- Harvest plums, gages, damsons, citrus, quince, olives, figs, apricots, cherries, peaches, nectarines, persimmons, myrtle and pomegranates.

Prune apples and pears in winter when it is easy to see the shape of each tree.

Wrap healthy apples in paper and store them somewhere cool and dry until wanted.

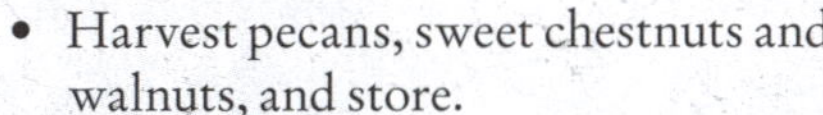

- Harvest pecans, sweet chestnuts and walnuts, and store.
- Move citrus plants back indoors or under glass. Start to reduce watering.
- Prune walnuts.
- Put grease bands around the trunks of fruit trees, to prevent attack by winter moth.

Soft fruit
- Remove the straw and old leaves from strawberries, and tidy up plants to expose the crowns to winter cold.
- Plant new strawberries.
- Continue to support melon fruit with netting or old tights; harvest fruit when ripe.
- Harvest grapes, blackberries and hybrid berries, autumn-fruiting raspberries, late-season and everbearer strawberries, goji berries, passion fruit, lingonberries and blueberries.
- Harvest kiwi fruit, then prune the fruiting shoots back to five leaves past the fruit so plants concentrate their energy in fruiting.
- Harvest cranberries, then trim the plants lightly.

WINTER
- Hoe out weeds around fruit plants regularly.
- Check all stored fruit and nuts regularly for rotting and disease.
- Order new bare-root bushes and trees.
- Prepare the ground and then begin planting new trees and plants.

Fruit trees
- Harvest citrus, and give plants a citrus feed. Prune at the end of the season.
- Check tree ties are secure and loosen if necessary.
- Prune apples, pears, medlars and quinces.
- Towards the end of the season, protect early stone-fruit blossom from frost with fleece.
- Prune cobnuts and filberts once their catkins are open.

Soft fruit
- Cut down all autumn-fruiting raspberry canes.
- Prune grapes.
- Prune black-, red- and whitecurrants and gooseberries.

Index

Page numbers in **bold** indicate a main illustrated section. Any other illustrations are indicated in *italic* numbers.

Quarto

First published in 2019 by Frances Lincoln,
an imprint of The Quarto Group.
One Triptych Place,
London, SE1 9SH,
United Kingdom
T (0)20 7700 9000
www.Quarto.com

This edition published in 2026 by Frances Lincoln.

EEA Representation, WTS Tax d.o.o., Žanova ulica 3,
4000 Kranj, Slovenia
www.wts-tax.si

A catalogue record for this book is available from the British Library.

ISBN 978-1-80570-033-3
Ebook ISBN 978-0-71124-718-5

10 9 8 7 6 5 4 3 2 1

Design by Sarah Pyke

Printed in Guangdong, China TT102025

Photographic acknowledgements
a=above; b=below; m=middle; l=left; r=right

© **Alamy** 8l John Glover, 14l Keith M Law, 20 Brian Hoffman, 23ar John Glover, 23bl Deborah Vernon, 29br Marting Hughes-Jones, 33rb Elizabeth Whiting & Associates, 35ar Tatyana Ivanikova, 138al wdo bravo, 141r Deborah Vernon

© **GAP Photos** 12 Friedrich Strauss, 23br Clive Nichols, 24al Jacqui Dracup, 24b GAP Photos, 29bl John Glover, 30r Visions, 35al+b GAP Photos, 43ar Friedrich Strauss, 55al Howard Rice, 55ar Carole Drake, 55br GAP Photos, 63al Graham Strong, 63ar+ml+mr+b GAP Photos, 75ml+mr GAP Photos, 91mr Jo Whitworth, 95ar+ml+mr+b GAP Photos, 138ar Carole Drake

© **Shutterstock** 2 Kostiantyn Kravchenko, 8r EsfilPla, 9 AVN Photo Lab, 10l Kostiantyn Kravchenko, 11a Nataliia Krasnogor, 11b Chadapa Chansang, 14r studiogi, 15l Cynthia Shirk, 15r kryzhov, 17 Fotokostic, 19 1JMueller, 23al photowind, 24ar Yunava1, 26 Elena Masiutkina, 27 Linda George, 29a Andrew Fletcher, 30l AXL, 31 Nadejda Zaharevskaja, 33l locrifa, 33ra YP Carol Woytila, 36–7 Kosikhina Anna, 38 Su Justen, 40 alybaba, 43al Genik, 43am Iness_la_luz, 43m Far_Away, 43b Piyada Jaiaree, 44 Rianna Nandan, 46 Valeri Potapova, 49al marketlan, 49ar AnnaDona, 49ml 13.20 Team, 49mr Reschme, 49b hiphoto, 50 aspen rock, 52 Carmen Sorvillo, 55bl Michele Ursi, 56 Jasminka Keres, 57 Evilka, 59 Andrew Fletcher, 61 photowind, 64 Peter Turner Photography, 65 Sup U, 66 nnattalli, 67 joserpizarro, 68 Iryna Loginova, 69 Lulub, 70 Nick Pecker, 73 Peter Turner Photography, 75al Minoli, 75ar Sergey Pozdyaev, 75b Brent Hofacker, 77 ThankYou ThankYou, 78 wolfness72, 80l Joanna Tkaczuk, 80r John Mobbs, 83al Africa Studio, 83am Katsiaryna Shpihel, 83ar rouille-et-patine, 83m 13Smile, 83b Africa Studio, 84–5 Belka10, 86 Jiri Vaclavek, 87 mcherevan, 89 nuchverywell, 91al Chongsiri Chaitongngam, 91ar Tortoon, 91ml FotoDuets, 91b Single, 93 paty, 95al Elena Masiutkina, 97 Orest Iyzhechka, 99al Lisaveta, 99ar Somporn Keatdilokrat, 99m xveron90x, 99bl aniana, 99br Studio Barcelona, 100 Tropical Daze Photography, 101 svf74, 102 Nick Pecker, 104a guentermanaus, 104b Elena Rostunova, 106 Nick Pecker, 108 Diana Taliun, 110 ch_ch, 111 M. Schuppich, 112 Kostiantyn Kravchenko, 113 MyTravelCurator, 115al Draw05, 115ar ivSky, 115ml Bildagentur Zoonar GmbH, 115mr Shebeko, 115b Gulsina, 116 Joanna Tkaczuk, 119 Joanna Tkaczuk, 120 Ruslan Kudrin, 121 Martins Vanags, 123 Valeriy Ermakov, 124–5 Igor_S, 126 Sergio Schnitzler, 127 Hector Ruiz Villa, 129al Bildagentur Zoonar GmbH, 129am ChiccoDodiFC, 129ar HelloRF Zcool, 129b from my point of view, 130 Martin Fowler, 133 Aleoks, 135 Viktoria Ivanets, 136l Scott Sanders, 136r Starover Sibiriak, 137l Henri Koskinen, 137r Radovan1, 138bl mariocigic, 138br Vadym Zaitsev, 141l ueuaphoto

© **Steven Wooster** 119tl+am+ar